# Running with God

## spiritual fitness for all seasons

KENNETH ROLHEISER

## Dedication

This book is dedicated to those close to me
who have finished the race,
and to my fellow runners who inspire me
and support my writing with their prayers.

Twenty-Third Publications
A Division of Bayard
One Montauk Avenue, Suite 200
New London, CT 06320
(860) 437-3012 or (800) 321-0411
www.23rdpublications.com

Copyright ©2006 Ken Rolheiser. All rights reserved. No part of this publication may be reproduced in any manner without prior written permission of the publisher. Write to the Permissions Editor.

The Scripture passages contained herein are from the *Jerusalem Bible*, copyright ©1966, Doubleday & Company, Inc. Used by permission. All rights reserved.

ISBN-10: 1-58595-574-4
ISBN 978-1-58595-574-9
Library of Congress Catalog Card Number: 2005936956
Printed in the U.S.A.

# Contents

|  |  |  |
|---|---|---|
|  | Introduction | 1 |
| Chapter 1 | Running toward Heaven | 3 |
| Chapter 2 | Running in the Cool Breezes | 14 |
| Chapter 3 | Running with Hungry Hearts | 23 |
| Chapter 4 | Running toward Holiness | 35 |
| Chapter 5 | Running with Repentance | 50 |
| Chapter 6 | The Road All Runners Come | 65 |
| Chapter 7 | Running to See God | 82 |
| Chapter 8 | Running beside the Cross | 91 |
| Chapter 9 | Running into God's Arms | 105 |

# Introduction

Earlier this spring as I was jogging among the trees, I felt inspired to challenge other "sexagenarians" to join the "race of life." I recalled the words of Psalm 92:

> Still bearing fruit when we are old,
> > still full of sap,
> > still green,
> > to proclaim that the Lord is just.

The sap is still running in the trees! I also recalled the words of Spanish poet, Antonio Machado:

> Traveler, the path is your tracks
> And nothing more.
> Traveler, there is no path.
> The path is made by walking.

If you join me on this journey, you may occasionally need to catch your breath, but the secret is to keep running. Our challenge is to live life with intensity! When we keep running the good race, the Spirit of God bears us up on eagle's wings; the breath of God lifts us higher and higher. With the Spirit working in us we can do awesome things. It is the Spirit who guides us and leads us to do God's will.

In *Running with God* I want to challenge you—and myself—to run toward God with the enthusiasm that befits our calling as Christians. I want to reflect on the challenges we all face as the seasons of our lives pass. Above all, I want us to have the joy of an enthusiastic day laborer in the vineyard of the Lord.

As a young man I spent one summer working on a general construction crew building a service station. Our foreman was an enthusiastic leader who inspired us by always jumping in to carry the biggest piece, to lift the toughest steel girder. We actually whistled as we worked (the tune is still in my head), and when we carried a piece of lumber from point A to point B, we ran. I do not exaggerate. (I still do this—run from time to time when working on a menial task—especially when the day is hot. My family sometimes jokes, "Who's shooting at you?")

*Running with God* attempts to recognize the touch and presence of God in our daily lives. God is present to us in the creation around us. "Look at the heavens and learn," Einstein said. Poet Bliss Carman in "Vestigia" took a day to search for God and found God's footprints in the scarlet lily, his voice in the song of the thrush, "his hand was light upon my brow."

Let us live our lives and tell our stories with the urgency of St. Paul:

> But life to me is not a thing to waste words on,
> > provided that when I finish my race
> I have carried out the mission the Lord Jesus gave me
> > and that was to bear witness
> > to the good news of God's grace. (Acts 20:24)

As we all know, our run through life passes through cloudy days and days when the wind blows against us. We will never reach our destination if we walk only on sunny days. And so, let us begin. As we run together in this good race, may the breath of God be the "wind at our backs" (to borrow from the familiar Irish blessing). Motivated by joy, may we run, not walk.

Let us "throw off everything that hinders us, especially the sin that clings so easily, and keep running steadily in the race we have started" (Hebrews 12:1–2).

## Chapter 1

# Running toward Heaven

*If you take two steps toward God,
God runs to you.*

—*Hindu saying*

Recently I was struck by the image of a figure departing and moving off in the distance. As the seconds passed, the figure seemed to disappear in increments, slowly dropping in stature, seeming to sink into time and distance. I realized that our lives are normally lived in such increments. We take perceptible steps into time and space. It can be observed and measured physically. There is no going back. From the moment of our birth we move inexorably toward the day when we will be born to eternal life. We start on the journey of life as children. With any luck, we will end the journey as "children" before God.

## Where Are We Going?

> *A young boy was running along a road. He was stopped by an adult who asked, "Where are you running to in such a hurry?" The boy replied, "I am on my way to heaven."*

What is it we are running toward if not a deeper relationship with God? If our relationship with God is not an exciting love affair we need to examine our part in it. God is Love and we know for sure that God loves us with an everlasting love. If love is lacking, the fault does not lie with God.

> **If our relationship with God is not an exciting love affair, we need to examine our part in it.**

It's something like this. A youngster gives his father this proposition: "Dad, if you give me a dollar I'll be good." The father answers, "Son, when I was your age, I was good for nothing." This little joke illustrates our perennial human problem. We have alienated ourselves from our heavenly Father by abandoning some of the great spiritual traditions of our fathers and mothers. Attending Mass, family prayer, religious symbols in our homes—all are reminders that God is with us. They remind us that we are running toward God every moment of our lives. Without such reminders we often feel despondent, maybe even despairing. Though we have not abandoned goodness, we seem to have despaired of a close relationship with God. How do we get it back?

In the poignant song "Dance with My Father," Luther Vandross expresses a deep longing to reconnect with his father. If he could, he would choose a song that never ends if only he could dance with his father one more time.

How long has it been since we "danced" with our heavenly Father? Certainly the saints experienced the closeness of a dance with God in the sense that they always saw themselves as children of God. God danced with them, tickled them, wrestled on the floor with them. Philip Neri, for example, often spent time before the Blessed Sacrament in church. He was so overcome with joy the other priests would find him on the floor laughing and saying, "Enough, Lord, I beg you! I can't take so much joy!" (*The Word Among Us*, February 2004).

Just as we once bathed our infant children, tickled them, and rolled on the floor with them, our heavenly Father longs to be with us, his children. He longs to love us. When we repent and come back to him, as Zephaniah (3:17–18) says:

> He will exalt with joy over you,
> > he will renew you by his love;
> he will dance with shouts of joy for you
> > as on a day of festival.

Somewhere and somehow many of us have lost our spiritual innocence, the innocence that allows us to be children before God. We need to hear again and experience again that God is Love and is waiting for us with open arms.

## Where Is God?

*The story is told of two naughty boys always in trouble. Their Sunday school teacher had the brilliant idea of putting the fear of God into them as a cure. So she consulted the priest and had him separate the two and deal with them one at a time.*

*He met with the younger one first and asked him, "Where is God?" The boy did not answer. "Where is God?" he asked again. Still no reply. He then asked a third time, "Where is God?"*

*The boy jumped up and ran out to his brother. "We are in big trouble!" he gasped.*

*"What's wrong?" asked the older brother, worried about what sin might have caught up to them.*

*"God is missing," said the youngster, "and they think we have something to do with it!"*

Is God missing in our lives today?

How much we fear judgment and condemnation from our God of love! Perhaps the "fire and brimstone" sermons of the past (at least in my childhood) are to blame. "Flee the hidden God and run to Christ," Martin Luther encouraged his students. Our God is not the hidden, unapproachable God of the Old Testament in which once a year on Yom Kippur the high priest was permitted to enter the Most Holy Place. He was not permitted to look at or touch the Ark of the Covenant on pain of death. A rope with a bell was tied around his ankle, so that if he made a mistake and died, his corpse could be dragged out.

## The God of Open Love

In contrast, the God that Jesus came to reveal is the God of open love. He is the father waiting for his prodigal son (Luke 15:11–32). God is watching for us, waiting for us, offering forgiveness and celebration at our return. I recall a lyric from the song "One of Us" by Joan Osborne: "What if God was one of us." Jesus came to reveal God to us. He came, in fact, to become (in Osborne's words) "a slob like one of us." He hung on the cross between two other "slobs." The term is used figuratively here; not in the sense of a stupid or untidy person, but in the sense that we are "mud," from the Irish origin of the word. God came down to earth to walk with us, to share the "mud."

A traditional belief about the thieves on the other crosses is that the thief on the right, to whom Jesus said, "This day you will be with me in Paradise," fared much better than the thief on the left. We even carry this idea into an ordinary card game, Sheep's Head, where the spade jack is known as the "left jack" and the club jack is the "right jack" and has more power. I submit that both thieves were in a privileged salvation position. God was one of them, one of us, that day. Jesus came to tear open the temple veil that separated them and us from God.

I take great consolation in our experience of the loving "Abba" revealed to us by Jesus.

I want a loving Father in whose hands I can place myself when things get really rough. An example comes to mind. In my teaching career, I can remember a time of great tension. The agony I felt robbed me of peace and sleep. Finally I prayed, "Lord, I put this in your hands. It is too much for me to carry." I managed to sleep that night, and the next day was not as tough as I imagined it would be. I want that same Father to be there at the end of my life when I say, "Into your hands I commend my spirit." Ecclesiastes (2:14) says: "The wise see ahead, the fools walk in the dark." At the end of the day, when I close my eyes, God, I want you to be there.

> At the end of the day, when I close my eyes, God, I want you to be there.

This present life is a time of transition. Christ must increase; we must diminish. We are heralds, signs to the world that God's love is breaking through in an unprecedented way. There are two billion Christians worldwide, and we have the structure of the church to be Christ's loving arms to the world. We must be those open arms to those around us: family, parish, community, and world. Our God is Love. Our God has open hands, not closed fists. Our God is a God of restraint. Just as Jesus died with open hands, all the while forgiving his tormentors, our God waits for us with open arms. Do we turn away or do we turn toward God? Our God loves us enough to give us the choice.

## On the Lighter Side

*One night during a violent thunderstorm: "Mommy, will you sleep with me tonight?"*

*"I can't, dear. I have to sleep with Daddy."*

*Then a shaky little voice, "The big sissy."*

Aside from this humor about fatherhood, there is great joy in actually being a father. I can only imagine how much greater yet God's joy must be! Our God is a God of joy who made the earth and made us and declared it very good indeed. Let's revel in this for a moment; it is cause for great joy. I believe that God awaits us with love, even if we have become alienated from him. At the beginning of this chapter, I quote the Hindu saying: "If you take two steps toward God, God runs to you." I truly believe this. Again, Scripture bears this out in Christ's parable of the Prodigal Son (Luke 15). "When the father saw him returning, he ran out to meet him." While it is still possible to return, let us take those two steps.

The *Pater Noster*, or Our Father, was given to us by Jesus to encourage us to praise the Father, ask forgiveness, and work for the coming of the kingdom by loving others. No other prayer is as universally recognized and loved by all Christians. It is a sign of the unity of all Christians who together make up Christ's body on earth. We are one big family on a journey toward God.

I know what a joy it is to have children grow and develop within a family bond whose love is strong enough to bring them back when they stray. As a father, I have witnessed the mistakes of their youth, and I have welcomed their recognition of those errors. Above all, I have always recognized that though they were flesh of my flesh, my children are a sublime gift from God. And God our Father is perfect in love! Through Jesus he revealed to us that his heart is that of a shepherd tenderly caring for the sheep (Matthew 18). God is also a passionate lover leaping over mountains and hills, rushing to embrace the beloved (Song of Songs 2:8–14). Rejoice and believe the good news!

In Hosea 2, the Father, who loves us even when we stray, says: "Come back to me…." When Israel (and that includes all of us, children of Adam and Eve) "forgot" the Lord, God pursued her: "I will allure her…she shall respond there as in the days of her youth. I will espouse her to me forever in love and in mercy."

Recently I was reflecting on the magnitude of God's love. I had been reading Colossians 1:15–20. "Now the Church [that's us] is his body, he is the head," the passage concludes. Jesus "holds all things in unity"; "For in him were created all things [us again] in heaven and on earth." Wow! This is a great starting point for understanding the nature of our relationship with God. What is behind the magnitude of God's love for us, God's eagerness to share his life with us—unworthy as we are? Why did God create us? It was indeed to share his love with us and to share his very nature with us. This nature was revealed to us by Jesus, God's own son.

Christ wants to make us one with himself and the Father. The eternal vision of the Father, knowing the cost of this sacrificial love, brought Jesus to earth as God-man. Why would God send his own son? Because he loves us that much. Jesus shared our joy and our suffering. He experienced the "blood and water" of humanity, even the temptation and fear and agony of Gethsemane and Good Friday. He could have kept an antiseptic distance, but he did not.

How does all this touch our lives? The commandment of Christ is clear: "Love the Lord your God" and "your neighbor as yourself" (Luke 10:27). At the Last Supper, he goes even further: "love one another as I have loved you" (John 13:34). We too must get into the blood and water of life, into its risks and insecurities, into its service of others. The more we become like Christ, the more aware we become of God's love for us.

## The Ultimate Symbol

The cross of Christ is the ultimate symbol of this love. We need its magnitude. We need something so great to trust in when temptation comes our way or we are facing trials or death. When we look at the cross, its saving power strengthens and helps us. The Israelites traveling in the desert were saved from the bite of poisonous snakes when they looked at the serpent on the pole (Numbers 21:9). In the New Testament, those who look at and believe in Christ on the cross are saved from the "bite" of death, sin, and spiritual weakness.

> Jesus seeks us still today. Even if we have strayed, the shepherd is seeking us.

We do not have to seek far and wide for what God gives us in our hearts: "The word is very near you; it is in your mouth and in your heart for you to observe" (Deuteronomy 30:14). Turn to the Lord in your need and you will live. "For the Lord hears the needy, and does not despise his own who are in bonds" (Psalm 69). These words encourage us to open our hearts to God and to embrace God's plan in our lives as Jesus did.

In many ways, the God of the Old Testament was a God to fear. Some of the stories are disquieting, to say the least. There is the story of the destruction of Sodom and Gomorrah, the flood of Noah, and countless stories where the prophets interpret disasters and defeats as punishment from God. The good news is that this is the God of the Old Testament, for Jesus came to reveal to us the Father's love and to offer us a new covenant.

Jesus tells us this comforting story.

> Which one of you, having a hundred sheep and losing one of them, does not leave the ninety-nine in the wilderness and go after the one that is lost until he finds it? When he has found it, he lays it on his shoulders and rejoices.…Just so, I tell you, there will be more joy in heaven over one sinner who repents. (Luke 15:1–10).

In countless ways Jesus tells us that he is the good shepherd and we are his sheep. The good shepherd lays down his life for his sheep. He faces the evil forces of the night to save the sheep.

Jesus seeks us still today, and at the end of the day he calls out to us: "Where are you?" Even if we have strayed, the shepherd is seeking us. Because of Jesus, our understanding of God has changed. In his parables, Jesus tells us about the love of a Father that we know well enough to call "Abba" or Daddy. We never need to hide from God because of our human nature and weaknesses. Our creator understands our human frailty and loves us in spite of it. It is time then for us to stand up and say, "Here I am Lord." It is time for us to enjoy regular strolls and visits with our God.

## We Are Privileged People

We are privileged to be disciples of Jesus and to have heard the message of salvation. "Happy the eyes that see what you see, for I tell you many prophets and kings wanted to see what you see, and never saw it; to hear what you hear, and never heard it" (Luke 10:23–24). Yet, because of our human nature we need real and frequent reminders about our spiritual heritage. One reminder came to me at the funeral of my father-in-law, Walter. My oldest brother remarked, "Walter was a very rich man." He was referring to Walter's faith and values. His wife and children were gathered to celebrate his goodness, to pay tribute to Walter's life of love, his "wealth."

Since that day I have often reflected on this, and I realize that my own father had such wealth. He did not leave many earthly treasures for his children, but he did leave a legacy of faith and values. As children of God, we are offered spiritual wealth. God's kingdom has no end, and we are its heirs. We can look forward to the great banquet prepared for us in God's kingdom, and every day of our lives we can be running closer and closer to it. "Now I confer a kingdom on you, just as my Father conferred one on me: you will eat and drink at my table in my kingdom" (Luke 22:29–30). How do we open ourselves to this kingdom? How do we share it with Jesus? "Anyone who does the will of my Father in heaven, he is my brother and sister" (Matthew 12:50).

Jesus came as a baby to Bethlehem to embrace our humanity and our experience, to relate to our condition. Jesus was born in a stable, going first to the poor and displaced. Shepherds were the first to hear the news. Christ lived, laughed, loved, and died in our world. He understands our suffering, our longings, and our needs. He understands, blesses, and loves us for the ways in which we are poor.

When Will We "Get It"?

> There once was a small town preacher who kept repeating the same sermon every Sunday morning. Finally, in exasperation, one of his timid flock approached him and asked, "How come you give us the same message week after week?"
>
> "Well," the minister said, "when I can see that you have caught on to this first lesson and that your lives have changed, then I will be able to go on to another message."

When will we catch on to the magnitude of God's love for us? When will we "get it"?

Just as Jesus called God "Abba" the way one would refer to a loving dad, we too can speak to God and in our hearts and call him "Daddy." I have absorbed this message in my brain. My head knows that I can talk to God this way, but my heart needs to accept the truth of it, the joy of it. "Abba! Daddy!" As the preacher above did, we need to repeat this message in our heads until our hearts believe and our lives reflect the change.

I still choke with emotion when I think of a saintly aunt of mine, an Elizabethan nun at Humboldt, Saskatchewan, dying of cancer. Like the nun crying out in the storm in Hopkin's "The Wreck of the Deutschland," in her last hours she repeatedly cried out, "Come, Jesus, come and get Sister Zita Rolheiser!" There is no possible way God could have ignored that repeated plea. She knew about the love of the heavenly Father. She was ready to let her life reflect that fact.

 For Your Reflection

*Let us love one another, for love comes from God. Whoever loves is a child of God and knows God. Whoever does not love, does not know God, for God is love. (1 John 4:7)*
- In what ways does your life echo this message?
- What change of heart would it take for you to be such an echo?

*If a shepherd has a hundred sheep, and one of them has gone astray, doesn't the shepherd leave the ninety-nine and go in search of the one that is lost? (Matthew 18:12)*
- Have you ever thought of God as searching for you?
- How does this make you feel?

*God has sent the Spirit of his Son into our hearts, crying, "Abba! Father!" (Romans 8:15)*
- What do you need most from God at this moment of your life?
- Spend time in prayer today calling, "Abba, Father!" Picture yourself running into God's arms.

Chapter 2

# Running in the Cool Breezes

I believe in miracles. I have to.

—*Terry Fox*

I remember my graduation day vividly. I spent one of the most boring hours of my life listening to platitudes and clichés, none of which I can recall today. What I do remember is gazing out the window of our parish hall and focusing on a well-worn cattle trail crossing distant green hills. That scene became a Camelot to me.

For many years I have remembered that image and all the promise it held in my young life. It was a trail sloping gently between green hills in the June sunshine. That trail is the path of life. In the morning and evening we can see the fresh dew drops and enjoy the calm. The mystery of what lies beyond this first hill can only be discovered by walking the path. At times the road leads uphill. At times the wind blows against us. At other times the slope goes gently downhill and the wind is at our backs. In the heat of the day the trail can appear to be hot and dusty, but oh, how we enjoy those morning and evening breezes!

No matter where our path of life leads or how busy we become, every day is better when we begin it in the cool breeze of God's presence. A simple Sign of the Cross dedicates the day to God. Our daily work is then imbued with God's presence and leads us to the cool of the evening, a time of peace in God's presence. Even if the only night prayer we can muster in our exhaustion is "Amen" and a Sign of the Cross, we will have offered an evening benediction for the gift of God's presence in our lives, and that will suffice.

When we begin and end our day with God, we have the light of life and we are safe, even when walking in the dark. "No evil will I fear, though I walk in the valley of the shadow of death" (Psalm 23).

Hope and Humor

*My brother, who is a farmer, once told me that I should carry a flashlight for protection against cows during calving season. "A cow may charge you if you get too close to her calf," he said. When I asked him how carrying a flashlight would protect me in the situation, he replied, "It all depends on how fast you carry it."*

We need to travel with "light" hearts. Hope and humor go hand in hand.

On the path of life, as long as God travels with us, we can keep hope in our hearts. The mystery of what lies beyond each hill is easier to accept when God walks with us, even when the road leads uphill. The great question is: how do we keep our life journey hopeful? How do we strive against all odds to achieve what is beyond our imagination?

Terry Fox struggled alone on a journey that started in St. John's, Newfoundland and ended just outside of Thunder Bay, Ontario, 5,373 kilometers in 143 days. He ran forty-two kilometers (twenty-six miles) a day, a marathon distance. More remarkably, he made this journey with an artificial leg, having lost his right leg to cancer two years before. His heart was light as he ran along, full of hope. He was running with a purpose, to get money for cancer research.

> The Holy Spirit will change us and make us new persons of hope.

Describing a particular run through Sparks Street Mall, Ottawa, he said, "People were lined up, clapping for me. I was just sprinting. I was floating through the air and didn't even feel a thing. I felt so great."

"I believe in miracles. I have to," Terry said. He had committed his life to his mission and proceeded with confidant joy. "For who wants to save his life will lose it; but anyone who loses his life for my sake…will save it" (Mark 8:35).

Terry's dream of running across Canada was never realized, yet he succeeded beyond his wildest dreams in achieving his goal of raising money for cancer research. The fundraising event Marathon of Hope was established in his honor. Thousands run more thousands of miles, and hundreds of millions of dollars have been raised for cancer research.

How do you and I continue our life-run with hope? I believe that we have a "cloud of witnesses" who cheer us on as we run the race of life. I am talking about our grandparents, parents, ancestors, and all those who have gone before us and have gained the crown of victory. They throng the sidelines and cheer as we continue on our lifetime run of hope. Jesus is first among them. When we respond to these cheers, we can achieve great things as Terry Fox did and as Hannah Taylor continues to do.

## Where Hope Can Lead

When Hannah Taylor was five years old she saw a man eating out of a garbage can. "I felt very, very sad," Hannah said later in an interview. "I asked my mom why the man was doing that and she said because he was homeless." Hoping that she could help the homeless, Hannah started collecting spare coins in old baby-food jars, which were painted red and black like good-luck ladybugs.

She inspired others to contribute. In four years, this child has raised over $500,000 for her Ladybug Foundation.

"I know some people are afraid of the homeless," Hannah says, "but they are great people, wrapped in old clothes with sad hearts. Love them like family. They need that most of all." Hannah has made a path where none existed before. She hoped she could help. She took action and she did help.

Because Jesus walks with us, we too can achieve the impossible. The Holy Spirit, the love of God in us, will change us and make us new persons of hope. Hope is what gives us the vision to reclaim our dreams when we have lost them. Even when there is much suffering and many obstacles in our path, we can succeed because we are not alone. When we walk with Jesus, we are a majority. Together, we are stronger than one individual. Yes, we have a "cloud of witnesses," but we also have each other. Let me illustrate this through the following experience.

My wife and I were going to Saskatoon to spend the weekend with our children. A day or two before we left, I had a dream. In it, my dad and mom were coming to visit me in Canora. I anticipated this chance to sit and visit with them and experience the emotional warmth that is at the heart of family love. Such was my dream. The reality is that my parents died before I even moved to Canora—and that was thirty-six years ago! Now I had before me another chance to visit with my family members. On this trip I experienced in a small but real way what the reunion with my parents will be like in heaven, and also what the support of my family gives me today. Such experiences sustain our hope and keep us running toward God.

After the resurrection Jesus came back to his disciples and to us. His message was simple: "Peace be with you." Then he shared with them how Scripture was fulfilled in his life, death, and resurrection. He told them, "I am sending down to you what the Father has promised…the power from on high" (Luke 24:37–49). With the grace of the Spirit, we are running the race of life that St. Paul talked about so frequently, especially at the end of his life: "I have fought the good fight to the end; I have run the race to the finish; I have kept the faith" (2 Timothy 4:7–8).

The incredible news of Jesus is that we need not fear nor be troubled. Our greatest fears and insecurities are like straw in comparison to the great love, trust, and fire of the Holy Spirit. The Spirit guides us in the way of Christ, which is love sustained by hope. Just as we experience the love of family, so, too, we are invited to be in the family of God whose love touches us daily, if only we have the eyes of faith to see it.

"The Eyes to See"
> *A writer arrived at the monastery to write a book about the Master. "People say you are a genius. Are you?" he asked.*
>
> *"You might say so," said the Master, none too modestly.*
>
> *"And what makes one a genius?"*
>
> *"The ability to recognize."*
>
> *"Recognize what?"*
>
> *"The butterfly in a caterpillar; the eagle in an egg; the saint in a selfish human being."*
>
> —Anthony de Mello, *The Prairie Messenger*, May 19, 2004

We can't let the sweat and the trail dust confuse us. We are in the race and the Master can recognize the saint in the sinner. Jesus chose to be one of us. We, in turn, can choose to journey with him: "Jesus, remember me, when you come into your kingdom."

Not only do we need to stay focused as we run the race of life, we need to be driven. This word always reminds me of an Andy Capp cartoon where a friend asks Andy, "Does your wife drive you to drinking?" "No," Andy replies, "she makes me walk."

Our spiritual lives need to be driven by the power of the Spirit. Then we will be motivated to do deeds both great and small, and our drive will not falter. How do we do this, how do we keep our spiritual engines running? An example comes to mind. Saul of Tarsus (later St. Paul) was "breathing threats and murder against the disciples of the Lord" (Acts 9:1). He was certainly motivated with all cylinders firing. As he approached Damascus, a light from heaven flashed around him and you know the rest of the story. He was converted and started working for Christ. Imagine that! What made Paul's conversion possible was the work of the Holy Spirit.

*The Spirit guides us in the way of Christ, which is love sustained by hope.*

Like Paul, we need to have the motivation and dedication of an Olympic athlete; we need to be converted by Christ. Our love for God must be a passion that drives us past other distractions. Our love for God must be a passion that is stronger than any other in our lives.

Once we experience the love of God, we will never want to leave it. We will be driven. This is the meaning of conversion. I have a brother in his seventies who is a priest. Recently he was out running when he passed a man who was walking. "I'm too old to run," the man said. "How old are you?" asked my brother. "Forty-seven." My brother, this runner of God, recently started a new challenge as pastor in a city, years after most of us would seek rest and retirement. With the help of the Spirit, he is still climbing new mountains. In Japan recently, while attending a conference on World Marriage Encounter, he literally ran up and down a mountain for his morning exercise. As family members and friends, we know what motivates him. It is the Holy Spirit who drives and motivates him, and he welcomes whatever comes up over the next hill.

## Training and Focus

Running the good race requires training and focus. A good runner will not look back for fear of being overtaken by a runner with more concentration. As Christians running the good race, we should not spend too much time looking back either. Our focus must be on going forward. Our sins and mistakes are behind us; our dreams and aspirations are before us.

In *Running the Race*, Reverend William Greiner relates the following story:

> On the prairies of Saskatchewan in Western Canada, we had a farm dog named Arctic. Several times a week, we had to drive three miles to town to buy groceries. As we drove along the dirt roads, Arctic would run behind or alongside our wagon. But he would never stay on the road. He had to run after every rabbit he saw. He had to stick his nose behind every gate. He had to jump over every fence. At every farm he had to chase every cat and every hen. If a dog barked at him, he had to bark back ten times. When Arctic finally arrived back from town in the evening, he was tired out, not from keeping his feet on the track, but from running all over the place.

Greiner is talking here about focus. He offers five good focus rules for the Christian "runner":

1. Remember the example of others who have run the race before us. His "star" athletes give this advice:

    Daniel: "Don't be afraid of lions."
    Noah: "Don't be afraid of the floods."
    Gideon: "Don't be afraid of overwhelming odds."
    Abraham: "Don't be afraid of impossibilities."
    Moses: "Don't be afraid of the 'Red Seas.'"
    Joshua: "Don't be afraid of walls."

2. Keep your legs on the move. Patiently move toward your goal like a distance runner does.

3. Keep your feet on the track. Don't take short cuts from the course that is set for you or you will lose the crown.

4. Keep your body free. Sin is the obstacle that slows our progress!

5. Keep your eyes on the goal. Greiner uses the example of the tightrope walker Blondin, who walked a slender rope stretched over Niagara falls by keeping his eyes on a silver star

placed on the far side. Just so, we need to keep our eyes on the goal, on Jesus who has run the race before us.

## Someone Carries Us

My Dad used to have a crack team of horses. One was a huge Clydesdale named Sullie; the other was a standard-bred named Tiny. One day Tiny was brought in from winter range to join Sullie in pulling our bobsled to an evening school concert—several miles away. On the way home that night, we were caught in a blizzard. The horses lost the trail, and our bobsled, with a dozen family members in it, was floundering in deep snow. Exhausted, Tiny fell three times, but Sullie gathered her strength and pulled not only our sled and its occupants, but also the tiny horse by her side. Sometimes we are the tiny horse falling, and Jesus is the Clydesdale who carries us.

## For Your Reflection

*Once the hand is laid on the plough, no one who looks back is fit for the kingdom of God. (Luke 9:62)*

- Do you look back—or forward? Resolve today to let the past be past.
- What hopes do you carry in your heart as you run this lap of your journey?

*As long as the day lasts I must carry out the work of the one who sent me; the night will soon be here when no one can work. (John 9:4)*

- What is the work you have been sent to do?
- Are you driven to do it? Why or why not?

*I have come to bring fire to the earth, and how I wish it were blazing already! (Luke 12:49)*
- What "fire" has God placed within you?
- How might you more effectively set this fire ablaze?

*Come to me, all you who labor and are burdened, and I will give you rest. My yoke is easy and my burden light. (Matthew 11:28–30)*
- Do you feel burdened by life right now?
- How can you tap into the rest Jesus wants to give you?

Chapter 3

# Running with Hungry Hearts

*When we turn to look at God,
we meet a gaze filled with love.*

"Something has existed since the beginning that we have heard, and we have seen with our own eyes…touched with our hands…the Word, who is life. [This] we are telling you so that you too may be in union with us, as we are in union with the Father and with his Son Jesus Christ" (1 John 1:1–3). John continues in Chapter 4: "Love one another since love comes from God. God is love. As long as we love one another, God will live in us. Anyone who lives in love lives in God."

What keeps us from the deep fulfillment promised in John's gospel? How do we find the faith-filled path that brings fullness to our hungry hearts? Do we honestly believe it exists?

## All in Your Outlook

*There was a father who had two sons; one was a pessimist and the other an optimist. For Christmas the father did an experi-*

ment with their presents. The pessimist opened package after package, his frown growing with each gift. Finally he asked, "What's the catch, Dad?"

The father then hurried to the other son's room where he had dumped a huge pile of manure. The boy was busily digging and getting more jubilant with each forkful. "Why are you so happy?" the father asked. His son shouted, "With all this manure, there's got to be a pony in here somewhere!"

We spend much of our adult lives with our hearts hungry, looking for the pony. When we were young, we dreamed dreams. Our lives were a song waiting to be sung. We were waiting, hoping, praying, and wishing. It was like waiting for a precious package to arrive in the mail. Each day we watched, but it did not arrive. Sometime later, other packages arrived that compensated somewhat for what we still longed for and were still missing.

I remember one particular night on the farm where I grew up ten miles from the hamlet of Cactus Lake, Saskatchewan. Some of my siblings had gone to a movie and I was not allowed to go because I was too young. I paced restlessly along the country road that passed right by our gate. I couldn't walk the twenty miles to the movie, but I wanted to. I remember going through the upstairs closets, searching pockets of old coats for possible coins. If I had money, maybe I would be closer to my goal.

As adults, some of us are still seeking, still uneasy, still restless, still incomplete, especially in our relationship with God. Somehow we feel we don't qualify to be at the banquet table of the Lord, at the feast that will fulfill all our desires. We still fear death and find it difficult to resign ourselves to our present lives and accept that this is what we are; this is what God meant us to be. Week by week we wait for some package to arrive that will fulfill our desires and longings. We seldom even realize that it is God we are waiting for. We do not do this well, this waiting for God.

## Having to Wait

One summer I was caught in a situation of waiting that forced me to reflect. I had locked myself out of my car and had to call my wife to bring a set of keys. She was walking, naturally. As I waited in the city parking lot, I tried to look inconspicuous. I sat on the car, leaned against it, and walked around. At length I started to think about the displaced persons among us who have to live on the street. For them it is not an hour's wait. And yet, how difficult it was to just stand and wait that short time.

> *Our hope is found in the silent moments of our lives.*

Have you ever read the play *Waiting for Godot*? I never liked the tedious repetition and the fact that nothing happens. Until recently, I had missed Samuel Beckett's brilliant symbolism. His two characters simply pass the time repeating meaningless routines as they wait for Godot. "Nothing is done," is repeated, and there is no place to go. Every place you are, you are still waiting. The only escape from the boredom will be when Godot comes.

How closely this existentialist play represents us, waiting for God. There is a need for personal decision in a world lacking purpose: existence plus choice equals destiny. Too often it seems there is nothing to be done. Only God's coming will save us. Our habits become a way to waste time as we wait. As one character in the play says, "All I know is that the hours are long, under these conditions, and constrain us to beguile them with the proceedings which…become a habit."

*Waiting for Godot* has many moments of silence. During this silence the audience starts to reflect on the tragic humor of existence. Godot never comes. Our hope is found in the silent moments of our lives. Here we miss or meet the God we are waiting for. Hopefully we have not filled our lives with the noisy repetition of meaningless activities (or habits) that may confuse us into thinking that God will never come.

## A Deeper, Fuller Life

How do we find the deeper, fuller life that God brings? How do we accept our insufficiencies and inadequacies? The same God who saw a restless little boy pacing and going through coat pockets for treasure is the God who watches over us today. God sees us as his children and he loves us. To him we are priceless treasures despite our sins and weaknesses. God sees our potential, our goodness, and our promise. When we turn to look at God, we meet a gaze filled with love.

All our hungry and deep desires find fulfillment only in God's love, which is powerful enough to go beyond all our needs and wants. "You ravish my heart with a single glance." (Song of Songs 4:9). We are the bride who merely glances at the groom, at God, who desires to be with us. We are the treasure God longs for. We spend too much of our lives being afraid. God would have it otherwise. Voltaire once wrote: "God is a comedian, playing to an audience too afraid to laugh." God's love for us is a cause for deep joy.

## What Love Sees

> An elderly woman and her grandson spent the day at the zoo. Children were waiting in line to get their cheeks painted by a local artist.
>
> "You've got so many freckles, there's no place to paint!" a girl in the line said to the little boy. Embarrassed, the boy dropped his head. His grandmother knelt down next to him.
>
> "I love your freckles. When I was a little girl I always wanted freckles," she said, while tracing her finger across the child's cheek. "Freckles are beautiful!"
>
> The boy looked up, "Really?"
>
> "Of course," said the grandmother. "Why, just name me one thing that's prettier than freckles."
>
> The little boy thought for a moment, peered intensely into his grandmother's face, and softly whispered, "Wrinkles."

There is a genuine truth to the love expressed in this story. The innocent child loves as God loves us, just the way we are. There is no such thing as an ugly baby! When the grandmother looks at her grandchild, she sees a gift from God. She looks with the eyes of God, with the eyes of love. When a man and woman look at each other as partners in love, they experience the words of the song: "I love you just the way you are." It is not a happy or lasting relationship if one spouse says, "I'll love you if you lose forty pounds."

The late theologian Hans Urs von Balthasar, once observed that when Jesus said, "Unless you become like little children," he was also referring to himself. Jesus, the Son of God, actually became a child and sought his Father's wisdom. Like a child, Jesus heard his Father and did his Father's will. If we are like children before God, God will guide us toward holiness.

## "Other-Worldly" Wisdom

Every romantic quest on earth remains somewhat unfulfilled, unattained. There is no complete fulfillment of all desires. We often seek with passion things that leave us still hungry and thirsty for more. The only way to complete happiness is following the course of wisdom that is "other-worldly." All the treasures of God are revealed in Christ (Colossians 2:3). The wisdom of God is also revealed through Jesus Christ. What is folly to humans (Christ on the cross) is true wisdom and eternal salvation. Only in the Lord is there a promise of complete fulfillment. Sometimes I think we have forgotten how to live in faith, how to love God and others. The quality of the spiritual life simply evades us.

Recently I delivered a meal to an elderly friend and neighbor and shared tea and a visit afterwards. "I don't know what I will do for the rest of the day," he said. I suggested a walk in the September sun, but he does not walk much any more. And it struck me that in his isolation he epitomizes the human struggle with loneliness and feelings of meaninglessness.

As a culture we have slowly set up roadblocks to friendship and community. We have evolved the "nuclear family" whose members have left their home community and family ties to carry on a job in isolation in some distant city or country. We have developed a fierce independence where people strive for their own homes surrounded by fences, hedges, and security systems. We no longer borrow a hedge clipper from our neighbor. We all have our own lawn mowers, garden cultivators, and independence. And we end up living alone and often dying alone. We have unlisted phone numbers, our own TVs (often in our own rooms separate from the family), and the internet. We don't want to be bothered by others and their unwelcome contact.

Before my parents had a television, we used to travel over the winter fields by sleigh to our neighbor's farm to visit and watch the Saturday night hockey game. And they welcomed us even though we were not even related to them. I used to have a friend who would pop in unexpectedly whenever he was passing by. If I was cutting the grass, I would stop the mower and we would relax with cool refreshment in the shade. I miss that friend and that lifestyle. Though our culture might discourage us from such simple acts of friendship and reaching out, our faith tells us that our daily relationships and our small ordinary activities are as important as ever. Unless we become like little children and once again recognize God's will in our daily lives—as Jesus did—we will miss powerful opportunities to grow spiritually. With faith, every action can be noble, every activity sacred and in harmony with the Creator's purpose.

Thomas Merton put it this way: "It is enough to be, in the ordinary human mode, with one's hunger and sleep, one's cold and warmth, rising and going to bed. Putting on blankets and taking them off, making coffee and drinking it. Defrosting the refrigerator, reading, meditating, working, and praying. I live as my fathers have lived on this earth, eventually I die. Amen."

## Inner Happiness

In this world we are all runners in the race that will end when our natural lives end.

Sometimes we are not sure of the way. Where can we satisfy our hungers and longings? Maybe the answer lies in more consciously exploring the source of inner happiness. Reaching out to others helps, but faith helps more. "Do you love me?" Jesus asks Peter in John 21:15. Picture for a moment the resurrected Christ sitting at your table and eating with you as he ate the bread and fish with Peter, Thomas, Nathaniel, and four others who had been fishing. But his question to you as he looks into your eyes is more pointed and more personal: "Do you love me more than these [others do]?" Inner happiness comes through our response to Christ's question. A wholehearted "yes" is the work of our lifetime. Every Sunday morning we again encounter Christ and this question. But often we don't appreciate this, and we don't answer.

## Hearing the Question

*The true story is told of a son who faithfully went to Sunday service each week with his mother. Eventually she died of old age. The next Sunday the now-aging son did not show up at church. The minister met up with him later and asked about it. "Oh," replied the son, "I don't have to go anymore. Mother is gone."*

What was the son doing all those years? Hadn't he ever heard Christ's question, "Do you love me?" Perhaps not.

I have a dear, dear friend who is fighting cancer, and he convinced the hospital to let him out for Saturday evening Mass. Christ's question is important to him. He values the opportunity to hear it, and he does his best to answer it. "Yes, Lord, I love you."

Richard Davidson, brain scientist, received a grant of $15,000,000 to study the effects of meditation on the mind. Among his subjects was the Dalai Lama who says, "cultivating happiness reduces suffering." Happiness is a skill that can be learned,

*We can make things better for ourselves through prayer and reflection.*

and it is not a luxury but a necessity. Davidson showed that people who are religious show more activity in the left side of the brain and are less likely to be depressed. Meditation can change the pattern of blood flow in the brain and produce a happier, healthier person. The Dalai Lama says, "We have the capacity to change ourselves because of the nature of the brain." In other words, we can make things better for ourselves through prayer and reflection.

A third and final time Jesus asks us, "Do you really love me?" Like Peter, we get many opportunities to get the answer right. It is not a trick question. Jesus loves us so much that he is inviting us to join him in a "giving" kind of love: "Feed my lambs." Yet we are more like Thomas than Peter. We doubt and we hesitate. Thomas would not believe unless he saw the risen Lord (John 20:26–29), but his hesitation gave us those encouraging words from Jesus. "Blessed are those who have not seen and yet have believed."

### Jesus, Help Me!

I recently read about Sister Briege McKenna, an Irish nun who was struck with rheumatoid arthritis that left her crippled and in a wheelchair. This happened at a spiritually "dry" time of her life. In desperation one day she closed her eyes and called out: "Jesus, help me." She felt a hand touch her. Opening her eyes she saw no one about. Then she realized she had been cured physically—all the stiffness and soreness were gone. More important, she felt a closeness to Jesus she had never known before (*The Word Among Us*, Easter 2004).

The point is that God can certainly work with our doubts. We need to call out in faith. Doubt can be a sign of faith, a sign that we are open to possibilities and to hope. A French philosopher once said that God is but a beggar who will not force us to believe. God invites us and calls us in the Spirit. Our response is to be open and ask for the gift of faith. With faith we can become instruments to show God's love to all the world.

When We Say "Yes"

> *God showed me a river and asked, "Will you give me your heart?" When I said "yes," I saw this lovely little white rose being thrown into the river. I watched the rose float downstream, carried by the flow of the water. I saw as it traveled along. People would stop and look at it as it passed them. People would smile when they saw the flower in the water. They would say, "Look at the lovely flower in the water."*
>
> *I saw when the flower went through an area that was ugly and dirty. I saw that the people there were sad and hopeless, and when they saw the lovely flower in the midst of all that gloominess and filth, it brought a smile to them, a look of hope to their faces. I understood then, if we will let God take our hearts and fill them with his river of love, letting that love flow through our lives, it will flow to many places, many people, making a difference in so many. It will bring joy, peace, and hope to the lives it touches.*
>
> —from the website Geocities.com

On one of our summer visits to my brother, my wife and I got our car stuck in the mud two and a half miles from the family farm. We walked in a steady rain and were thoroughly soaked by the time we arrived. My brother's quick wit sized up the situation, and he approached me with a glass of water. "Are you completely soaked? Wet through and through?"

"Yes," I replied.

"Well then this won't hurt you," he said, and splashed the water into my face. He was right. I was as wet as I could get. There was something very liberating about this experience (which in a normal situation might be upsetting). Why would I mind a little more water?

In much the same way we are "soaked" by God. In baptism, the Holy Spirit immerses us into the life of God, completely soaking us. "When we invite Jesus to come more deeply into our lives, we allow the Holy Spirit to rain down on us….Over a period of time—indeed, over the course of our lives—the Spirit reaches ever deeper into our hearts. Just as the rain comes regularly and nourishes the field, the Spirit wants to come into our hearts to nourish us with Jesus' healing and purifying love" (*The Word Among Us*, January 2005).

### A Dramatic Change

Being baptized in the Spirit brings about a radical change in us. Even the baptism of Jesus by John, an action one would think unnecessary, brought about a dramatic change. Matthew (3:16) describes this: Heaven was opened and he saw the Spirit of God descending like a dove and coming down on him. And a voice spoke from heaven, "This is my Son, the Beloved; my favor rests on him." Then Jesus began his public ministry and worked signs and wonders. After this nothing was the same for him. When we surrender to the Spirit, our lives too will change. The power of grace in us will be limitless, and we will never be the same again.

Imagine being immersed in the living waters of baptism. Now imagine someone splashing more life-giving water on you. That is the sense of abundance that can be ours in the Spirit. The living water will refresh us as the rain brings life to the trees and flowers. With the abundance of God's grace in our lives comes the call to discipleship. Just as he spoke to Peter inviting him to minister, Jesus calls us to "feed my lambs, feed my sheep." The graces and opportunities Jesus gives us are boundless. With his grace we are no longer impoverished. We will never be the same again. His love touches us and we are changed forever. Let me close with a beautiful story about the power of love.

We were the only family in the restaurant. When I sat Erik in a highchair he started squealing with glee and yelled, "Hi." He pounded his fat baby hands on the highchair tray, and he wriggled and giggled with merriment.

I looked around and saw the source of his joy. It was a man whose pants were baggy and whose toes poked out of worn-out shoes. His shirt was dirty and his hair was uncombed and unwashed. We were too far from him to know, but I was sure he smelled. His hands waved and flapped on loose wrists. "Hi there, baby; hi there, big boy." My husband and I exchanged looks, "What do we do?" The man was obviously drunk. My husband and I were embarrassed. When we finally got through the meal, my husband went to get the car. The old man sat poised between the door and me.

I turned my back trying to sidestep him, but as I did, Erik leaned over and reached with both arms to be picked up. Before I could stop him, Erik had propelled himself from my arms to the man's. In an act of total trust, love, and submission, he laid his tiny head upon the man's ragged shoulder. The man's eyes closed, and I saw tears hover beneath his lashes. He cradled my baby's bottom and stroked his back. He rocked and cradled Erik in his arms and then his eyes opened and set squarely on mine. "God bless you, ma'am, you've given me my Christmas gift." With Erik back in my arms, I ran for the car. My husband was wondering why I was crying and holding Erik so tightly, and why I was saying, "My God, my God, forgive me."

—Source Unknown

 For Your Reflection

*This is my Son, my beloved, my favor rests on him. (Matthew 3:16)*
- Can you imagine God saying similar words to you?
- In what ways do you feel "beloved" by God?

*Do you love me more than these? (John 21:15)*
- How would you respond to this question from Jesus?
- How does it make you feel to be asked?

*Feed my lambs. Feed my sheep. (John 21:15–17)*
- In what ways do you respond to this invitation from Jesus?
- What graces have you received to help you "feed" others in his name?

*My God, my God, forgive me. (story about Erik)*
- Have you missed opportunities to share what you have with others?
- You still have such opportunities, so how might you take advantage of them?

Chapter 4

# Running toward Holiness

*Like someone running a race, I try hard to reach the finish line so that I will receive the prize.*

—*Philippians 3:14*

Are you a mystic on your way to becoming a saint? Is the seed of holiness within you? Are you running so as to receive the prize? If you are reading this, chances are that you want to have a deep personal relationship with God. It is the nature of a seed to grow even if it falls on sand, on rocks, or among thorns. The seed that falls on good ground springs up and yields a "bumper crop." Jesus used this comparison in Mark 4:1–9. So a "number one" principle in our relationship with God is that our inner spiritual life, our mystic capacity, can grow. We can be mystics and saints.

## Aiming High

*A Catholic priest and a rabbi were chatting one day when the conversation turned to a discussion of job descriptions and pro-*

motion. "What do you have to look forward to in way of a promotion in your job?" asked the rabbi.

"Well, I'm next in line for the monsignor's job," replied the priest.

"Yes, and then what?" asked the rabbi.

"Well, next I can become a bishop," said the priest.

"Yes, and then?" asked the rabbi.

"If I work really hard and do a good job as Bishop, it's possible for me to become an archbishop," said the priest.

"OK, then what?" asked the rabbi.

The priest, beginning to get a bit exasperated replied, "With some luck and really hard work, maybe I can become a cardinal."

"And then?" asked the rabbi.

The priest was really starting to get annoyed now and replies, "With lots and lots of luck and some really difficult work and if I'm in the right place at the right time and play my political games just right, maybe, just maybe, I can get elected pope."

"Yes, and then what?" asked the rabbi.

"Good grief!" shouted the priest. "What do you expect me to become, God?"

"Well," said the rabbi, "One of ours made it!"

While being pope is not an option for us, becoming God-like is. Through baptism in Christ we are asked to direct our everyday existence onto a path walked by the children of God, as brothers and sisters of Christ. We are directed to the path of holiness where we stand every chance of "receiving the prize." We are invited to be mystics and saints.

"I could never be a mystic," most of us might think. Great mystics in the church are rare and have been celebrated through the centuries. John of the Cross, Therese of Lisieux, and Mother Teresa come to mind. But all of us have a relationship with "mystery," a relationship with the "hidden" God. We think about God; we are baptized into "oneness" with God's Son; and we eat the bread of

Christ's body in the eucharistic encounter. By all definitions and logic we are mystics. The only question is about the degree of our realization of what in fact "already is."

Theologian Karl Rahner wrote about us when he said, "the devout Christian of the future will either be a 'mystic'…, or will cease to be anything at all." "Mystic" comes from the Greek word *mystikos*, meaning "hidden." As Christians it is our nature to seek a personal relationship, a oneness with the hidden God revealed to us by Christ.

> Our union with God is a mystery.

Have you ever been in love? As a young man I can vividly recall being enthralled as I walked beside the young lady I was falling in love with. The wind was tossing her hair. All nature seemed to worship at her feet. Only one word can truly depict what was happening to my heart and soul: passion. A passion was growing. That passion continues to sustain our relationship after more than thirty-five years of marriage.

### A Passion for God

Similarly, our relationship with God must have passion. There is restlessness in our hearts that can only be resolved when we are in union with God. The emptiness inside can only be filled when we become one in Spirit with God. The human passion and love for a spouse achieves oneness and fulfillment as two become one flesh. Just as the union of man and woman has a spiritual dimension in love, so, too, our union with God is a mystery. This is what the Church teaches. "Spiritual progress tends toward ever more intimate union with Christ. This vision is called 'mystical' because it participates in the mystery of the Holy Trinity. God calls us all to this intimate union, even if special graces or extraordinary signs [seeing visions, hearing voices] are granted only to some" (*Catechism of the Catholic Church*, #2014).

I'm sure that if most of us went for an examination of our spiritual progress, we would learn that we aren't nourishing ourselves properly for the spiritual life.

## On the Humorous Side

*A guy walks into his doctor's office with a carrot stuck in his ear and an asparagus spear dangling from his nostril. "Doctor, I feel terrible," he says. "What's wrong with me?"*

*"I'm not sure," says the doctor, "but I can tell you're not eating right."*

We don't always make the best use of God's spiritual gifts to us. It may even be hard for us to recognize what the "food" for the soul is. What keeps us from God's loving and healing touch is not so much our stubborn pride as it is a sense of our unworthiness. We do not think God could love someone so imperfect. Yet Scripture abounds with examples that disprove this assumption. Jesus heals in situations of doubt, discouragement, and unbelief. Look again at the apostle Thomas. Jesus waited eight days before appearing to him after the resurrection. During this time Thomas heard about but did not believe the accounts of the other disciples. After his encounter with Jesus, however, Thomas, infused by the Holy Spirit, became a model for believers.

Jesus often sought out sinners like the Samaritan woman at the well (John 4:7). Though she is living in sin, her encounter with Jesus changed her and she hurried off to tell others in her town about the Messiah. Then there is Levi, the tax collector at whose house Jesus dines (Luke 5:29). When the Pharisees saw Jesus there they asked, "Why do you eat and drink with tax collectors and sinners?" Jesus said in reply, "I have come to call not the righteous but sinners to repentance." And don't forget the adulterous woman (John 8:11) whom Jesus does not condemn but heals with the words, "Go and sin no more."

Faith is a matter of accepting that God loves us in spite of our sinfulness. Humbly opening the door to the Spirit, God's loving grace leads us to holiness. We keep this door open through our daily prayer and reflection. Scripture reading and meditation, morning and evening prayers, prayers at mealtimes, the daily Prayer of the Church (usually recited by clergy and religious in the morning and evening), meditation on the rosary—all help open our hearts to the Spirit. A disciplined, healthy prayer life will keep us in touch with God's love.

We need not be ashamed to pray, even in public. Saying prayers before meals in a restaurant or saying our beads on the bus can be natural parts of our daily prayer. It is refreshing to see major league baseball players make the Sign of the Cross publicly, letting us know that they depend on God as they play ball. Once I was privileged to observe the oldest surviving member of the holocaust, a ninety-six-year-old man who had survived Dachau's infamous concentration camp. As I watched him facing east, wearing his yarmulke (cap) and Tallit (shawl) and saying his prayers in a hospital bed, I realized that I was witness to a special moment of grace. He was not embarrassed by his prayer but rather enriched by it.

As disciples of Jesus, we gather weekly with others for the memorial celebration of the Eucharist. In this very public way, we are spiritually nourished; we pray for the community and the world, and we go forth in peace to bring about the kingdom of God. We can only effectively proclaim the kingdom if we have undergone a conversion ourselves and are convinced of the good news. When we follow Jesus' invitation to repentance, forgiveness, and discipleship, we are experiencing the result of our daily and weekly prayer and reflection.

What is there about Christianity that makes us want to "buy into" the package? What is the promised "pay off"? In this world where pain, suffering and despair are so prevalent, we have to look for a deeper meaning to our existence, one that will ultimately lead us to great joy.

## Why Jesus Came

A pastor asked a Sunday school class, "Why does Jesus come at Christmas?" Without hesitation a four year old called out, "To make joy real." In a profound way this child hit the nail on the head. The seasons of Advent and Christmas point the way to the everlasting joy we look forward to as Christians.

Reccently I attended the very sad funeral of a teenager who had been in my confirmation class. He had committed suicide. I had been asked to say a few words during the service.

"Why do we continue to hope in Jesus?" I asked. "Because he is the Good Shepherd who looks for the one lost sheep of the ninety-nine. When he finds that sheep, he puts it on his shoulders and carries it back to the flock and there is much rejoicing. We don't feel like rejoicing now because we are still in the flock and lack the vision of eternal things. But someday we will see and someday we will rejoice with our loved one in the presence of the Shepherd who guides us all and loves us with an eternal love."

As I stood at the graveside, I realized that I couldn't even imagine the pain the boy's parents and siblings must have felt. I was profoundly moved by their loss. Yet in my heart I knew that my hope, our hope, is fixed on a future time when we can again share joy with our loved ones who have died. "The Lord God will wipe away the tears from every cheek" (Isaiah 25:8).

We need a great deal of convincing that Jesus is real. Why aren't we sure? Even John the Baptist sent word to Jesus, "Are you the one who is to come, or are we to wait for another?" Jesus answered them, "Go and tell John, the blind receive their sight, the lame walk, the lepers are cleansed, the deaf hear, the dead are raised, and the poor have the good news brought to them" (Matthew 11:2–5). After this John the Baptist was convinced that Jesus was the Son of God, "taking away sins" and performing all these signs. Are we that sure? Are we, like John, proclaiming it to the entire world? Our job is to continue the work of John, the work of Jesus. Every day we pray, "Thy kingdom come," and by following Christ we work to make it so.

Every day we need to focus on what it is that brings us joy. Our lives and daily struggles often lack the pure joy of a blind man who receives his sight, a lame person who can suddenly walk, a deaf person who can hear again, or one who hears the good news of the gospel. Our life's journey must include a vision of the joy we wait for in God's kingdom. That day we will exalt and we will rejoice in God who has saved us (Isaiah 25:9). All will be "joy and gladness, and sorrow and sighing shall flee away" (Isaiah 35:10).

> Every day we need to focus on what it is that brings us joy.

God is present at "ground zero" in our daily lives. We experience God when we experience and share love. God is love! The gifts of creation are ours from this loving God. Joy is a gift that sometimes eludes us when we forget the simple spiritual facts.

## What Is Greater?

Here's an email puzzle sent to me by a friend:

What is greater than God?
More evil than the devil?
The poor have it.
The rich need it.
And if you eat it, you will die?

This question was asked of a cross section of the population. Eighty percent of the kindergarten children got it. Seventeen percent of Stanford University students got it. (I didn't get it!)

The answer is "Nothing."

The late Henri Nouwen embraced a simple lifestyle when he left his brilliant career as a professor of spirituality at Harvard for L'Arche, a community founded by Jean Vanier. It was a challenge to leave his former life to simply "be" with the handicapped in the community of Daybreak, near Toronto. Nouwen describes leaving his "security as a critical observer" to jump into the unknown. The most difficult task, Nouwen discovered, was to give his life over to God's will. The challenge was to become a simple "repentant son" and to renounce the securities of what this world values. Shortly before his death, Nouwen wrote that he believed God was faithful and would give us the welcome and love we seek. He believed that God's love would gladden our hearts and fulfill our deepest desires.

Mother Teresa also believed this. She saw God everywhere and she met God in one person at a time. For her, sainthood was not a complicated process. She knew that we don't just "leave space" for God in our lives. All the space in our lives is God's space. Saints like these have a sense of urgency. Today is the day. We need to seek that which is life-giving now.

## The Opposite of Urgency

*The story is told of a resident in a Russian city some years back who went to an electrician and asked, "Can you come to my house and repair the wiring so I will be able to switch the power back on?"*

*"Well," said the electrician, "I can come two years from now on September 5."*

*"Will that be in the morning or the afternoon?" asked the resident.*

*"I don't see what possible difference it could make," said the electrician. "That is two years from now. But I can come first thing in the morning."*

*"Good," said the resident, "because the plumber is coming in the afternoon."*

We don't put off fulfilling our physical needs and desires. Who would tolerate it? But there is a certain relaxation and ease when it comes to our spiritual lives. We will go to Mass again sometime in the future. Grace before meals is a good idea when we get to it.

Someday, when we have extra money, we will remember those in need. The list goes on, but it is not an urgent "to do" list. But our salvation is something of today, not tomorrow. When Jesus announced his public ministry after reading from the scroll of Isaiah, he said, "Today this Scripture passage is fulfilled in your hearing" (Luke 4:21). We express this urgency when we pray: "Give us this day our daily bread." We would hardly be asking for something to eat for next month if we had nothing in the cupboard right now. Our spiritual choices and our need for conversion are just as urgent. Again and again, we need to turn to Christ and ask for faith, for the gift of the Spirit: "I want to believe, help my unbelief!" (Mark 9:24).

So many times in Acts we see that the Spirit came down on the disciples to strengthen and inspire them. It is not a one-time thing. In Acts 4:31, the Spirit gives them boldness. In 4:8, Peter is filled with the Spirit to give bold witness. In Acts 2:4, the disciples are filled with the Holy Spirit and speak in foreign languages. In 19:6, Paul lays hands on the disciples and they are filled with the Spirit. The key is that we ask; we dispose ourselves to the Spirit, open to the spiritual gifts and blessings God has for us, and open to a change of heart.

Being open to conversion is much like writing a book. We start with a goal and a thesis we want to develop. There is much tedious work in the details, and the daily pages may wear down our spirits. The sheer length of it overwhelms us. It tempts us to goof off at times, knowing that the deadline is very distant. But our spiritual conversion is the book of a lifetime! It has our sweat and blood in it. How can we settle for something second rate? The days and weeks and months go by, and the distractions keep coming. We need passion and intensity to resist them. A great book, like a truly spiritual life, does not come about without constant and diligent effort.

The secret to writing the greatest story is to tap into the best resources. As followers of Christ we can expect miracles, and we can

> It sometimes takes a leap of faith to believe that Jesus understands our nature.

travel down the road of life fully expecting to be cured. And there is so much at our disposal: the word of God, the cross that consistently reminds us that the greatest love forgives us, the Eucharist that is our nourishment, and the church that guides and safeguards our journey from baptism to resurrection. We need to frequent the wellsprings of life that inspire our journey and energize us for the long haul.

Let me share an experience of being in touch with the author of our journey. I was going through a trying time and was not sure how the next part of my "trip" would turn out. Roadblocks were stopping me, and I couldn't see a solution. I prayed. I asked others to intercede for me: my parents and a favorite sister (who have gone before me to eternal life), and Mary, the mother of Jesus. What struck me was the clarity of the answer I received as I prayed. I remember the inner voice telling me clearly three times (in case I was not sharp enough to pick it up the first time): "It will be all right. It will be all right. It will be all right." I started to relax and believe, and in time it was all right.

### Jesus Knows Us

It sometimes takes a leap of faith to believe that Jesus understands our nature. When he views us in our day-to-day life he knows what we are. I was observing my cat recently. She was cleaning herself, going through natural animal movements. I did not hold it against her that she is a cat, completely self-centered and self-indulgent. And I thought about the Lord watching me in a similar way. Jesus knows my nature and he understands it better than I do. He knows my physical and emotional needs and struggles. He had them himself. He still remains completely open to me. He loves and accepts me completely.

Romans 8:1 tells us there is no condemnation for those who are in Christ Jesus. In verses 3–4, Paul says there is no judgment on us, no sentence against us, and no damnation awaiting us. For those in whom the Holy Spirit dwells, everything we deserve under the law was set aside by Jesus' death and resurrection. The Holy Spirit brings life both to our spirits and to our bodies. Yet, living a life of faith and being open to daily conversion is easier said than done. The hope of resurrection does not eliminate our times of doubt and insecurity.

## Do You Really Believe?

*A man who was stretching a rope across Niagara Falls. When he finished he approached another man and asked, "Do you know who I am and what I am doing?"*

*"No," the other replied.*

*"I'm a tightrope walker. Do you believe that I can walk across that cable?"*

*"No," the man replied. So the tightrope walker went across on the cable and back again.*

*"You did it!" said the man.*

*"Do you believe I can walk out into the middle of the cable and do a cartwheel on the cable?" asked the performer.*

*"No, I don't believe you can do it," said the man. The tightrope walker executed the feat and returned.*

*"You did it!" said the man.*

*A third time the performer asked, "Do you believe I can go out onto the middle of the cable and juggle these three balls?"*

*"I don't believe you can do that," said the man. Again the feat was accomplished.*

*"You did it!" said the man.*

*Then the performer picked up a wheelbarrow of potatoes and asked the man, "Do you think I can push this wheelbarrow across the cable to the other side?"*

*After a pause, the man said, "I believe you can do it. You were able to do the other three."*

*"Are you sure?" asked the performer.*

*"Yes, I'm sure," said the man.*

*So the tightrope walker dumped the potatoes out of the wheelbarrow and said to the man, "Get in."*

Today Jesus is challenging us to get into the wheelbarrow. We have witnessed his miracles: feeding thousands, the miraculous catch of fish, walking on water, raising Lazarus from the dead, and many others. He asks us to believe so that we can experience his joy, peace, and hope.

Recently I was praying for some close family members and friends who no longer go to Mass and perhaps don't enjoy the regular peace, joy, and hope that they once did. Then it dawned on me: even God will not interfere with our free will! We can pray for others and encourage them, but it is up to them, as it is up to us, to make the right choices and enjoy the peace of God.

In another sense we can choose for our loved ones and assure that they are bound to Christ in love. As my brother Ron puts it:

> To love another person is to assure him or her a place (if he or she wants it) in heaven....We are the body of Christ on earth and, like Jesus, have the power to bind and loose. Among other things, this means that when our loved ones (spouses, children, family, friends, colleagues) no longer walk the path of explicit faith and church with us, we can connect them to the faith, the church, the body of Christ, and heaven itself simply by remaining bonded with them in love and community. By being connected with us, they are connected to the church (since we are the church). Moreover, when we forgive them anything, including their non-church going, they are forgiven by the church and forgiven too, Jesus assures us, in heaven. (*The Tidings*, October 15, 2004)

As a youth I was often filled with absolute joy and peace as I left church on Sunday morning. I still feel this way today. It is a joy the

Lord asks me to share with others. I know how unworthy I am. Like Peter, I sometimes say, "Go away from me, Lord, for I am a sinful man" (Luke 5:9). I also remember Isaiah, whose mouth was purified with a burning coal when he confessed his unworthiness. Then he heard the Lord ask, "Whom shall I send?" Isaiah replied, "Send me" (Isaiah 6:8). With conversion comes mission. If we really believe the miracles of Jesus, we are ready to get into the wheelbarrow, as long as Jesus is the one asking us to.

### Do You Trust God?

*A man slipped over the edge of a cliff and was left hanging onto the root of a tree, dangling over a sheer drop. He called for help and a voice answered him saying, "This is God."*

*"Can you help me?" called the man.*

*"Certainly," said God. "Just let go and I'll catch you."*

*The man hesitated, then called out, "Is there anyone else up there?"*

One of my favorite examples of a real and audible message from God is the call of Samuel (1 Samuel 3). Samuel is lying down in the temple when he hears his name called. He gets up and goes to Eli, saying, "Here I am!" Eli says, "I did not call; lie down again." This happens three times. Finally Eli figures it out and says, "If God calls you again, you shall say, 'Speak, Lord, for your servant is listening.'" The Lord does come and calls Samuel again. And Samuel says, "Speak, for your servant is listening." Samuel grew up to be a trustworthy prophet and "let none of his [the Lord's] words fall to the ground. And all Israel...knew that Samuel was a trustworthy prophet of the Lord."

We should not be surprised when God speaks to us. An even greater challenge is when God prompts us to speak for him. It might be to correct someone, or to speak out for justice, or simply to invite someone back to the family or church. We need to trust that we are worthy to be the messenger or prophet of the Lord.

> We know that when God speaks, things happen.

(God even spoke through a donkey once, in Numbers 22:28!)

Have you ever heard God's voice? Usually we hear it as an inner prompting that we have learned to listen for. It tells us right from wrong or prompts us to do good things:

"Go visit John in the hospital."

"Go to Mass and pray for the family."

"Be calm."

"Don't believe that story!"

We know that when God speaks, things happen. In Genesis, God spoke and the whole creation came into existence. God spoke and the Israelites were set free. God called his people to repentance through the prophets. In the book of Jonah, God spoke to Jonah, who tried to dodge the call. Eventually Jonah went to Nineveh and warned the city, and the people repented. Jonah was disappointed that his prophecy of destruction was nullified, and he sulked. God created a castor-oil plant to give him shade and Jonah was delighted with the plant. But the next day God arranged that a worm attack the plant and it withered. Jonah was "steamed" again, or maybe "scorched" is a better word, as the sun beat down on him. God pointed out that Jonah was unhappy to have one plant destroyed. Yet he wanted God to destroy a great city of 120,000 people.

Praised be the Lord, the God of compassion for calling us to conversion. Not only does God give us a great deal of time and opportunity for grace to work, but also sends prophets to herald the good news. And remember, the Holy Spirit is always in our hearts to prompt us when we need stirring.

 For Your Reflection

*I have come to call sinners, not the righteous, to repentance. (Mark 2:17)*
- In what ways are you in need of repentance?
- Do you think of yourself as a sinner, who, in spite of sin, is called to holiness? Do you believe Jesus can transform you?

*All will be joy and gladness, and sorrow and sighing shall flow away. (Isaiah 35:10)*
- Do you look forward to the time you will experience such joy and gladness?
- Do you feel apprehensive about this time?

*I want to believe, help my unbelief! (Mark 9:24)*
- Do you pray daily for a deeper faith?
- Do you believe that God can make you a saint?

*Speak, Lord, your servant is listening. (1 Samuel 3:10)*
- Are you, like Samuel, listening for God's call?
- In what ways is God asking you to "keep running" for the prize?

# Chapter 5

# Running with Repentance

The race belongs not only to the swift and strong but also to those who keep running.

*—based on Ecclesiastes 9:11*

Imagine how free, happy, and unburdened we would feel to be forgiven and at one with the Lord! Christ himself invites all of us to this spiritual place: "Come to me, all you that are weary and are carrying heavy burdens, and I will give you rest. Take my yoke upon you, and learn from me; for I am gentle and humble in heart, and you will find rest for your souls. For my yoke is easy, and my burden is light" (Matthew 11:28–30).

## God Spoke First to Shepherds

*The old shepherd said to the other shepherds: "Imagine! An angel talking to us! None of the uppity-ups in this town would lower themselves to talk to us, but an angel did, and the child is right here in a stable where we can go and see him." As he*

*spoke, rivulets of tears were inching down the shepherd's weathered face.*
—from "The Cradle, a Christmas Story" by Ralph F. Wilson

The true story of Christmas is always touching and joyful. The heavens opened that night and joy was boomed to a startled earth: "Glory to God in the highest, and peace to his people on earth" (paraphrase from Luke 2:14). The angel echoes the news: "Behold I bring you tidings of great joy" (Luke 2:10). "Rejoice and believe the good news" becomes "Repent and believe the good news." "The people that walked in darkness have seen a great light; on those who live in a land of deep shadow a light has shone, for there is a child born for us, a son given to us" (Isaiah 9:1–6).

We have all this good news, but when it comes to repentance, we don't seem in a hurry. Why is this? Why do we let weeks, months, and even years pass without tapping into the joy of God's presence? We have the Mass, the sacraments, prayer, and Scripture, but we aren't urgent about using these means to draw closer to God. We are like the hare, sitting and resting during the race of our lives, while the turtle plods steadily along toward the finish line. Why don't we keep running?

As I ask this question, I am struggling with the news that a close friend of mine has just been "born to eternal life." I am at the age where this kind of event occurs frequently. I am visiting friends in hospitals and in senior housing on a regular basis now. That is good news for me in a spiritual sense, because I am constantly reminded of the ultimate meaning of life and the loving arms of a Father who calls and welcomes all of us in due time.

When Mary was with child she went with haste to a town in the hill country of Judah to visit Elizabeth. When Mary greeted Elizabeth, John the Baptist, the child in Elizabeth's womb, leaped for joy. Elizabeth gave a loud cry and said, "Of all women you are the most blessed, and blessed is the fruit of your womb. Why should I be honored with a visit from the mother of my Lord?" (Luke 1:39–43). Mary and Elizabeth knew the urgency of that sacred moment, and they were fully open to it. We all have sacred moments. With very little effort we can turn to the Lord in our daily lives! With little effort we can celebrate God's presence in our parish community on Sunday mornings. But we wait; we hesitate.

## More Joy in Heaven

The Lord is loving and patient. In his well-known parable (Luke 15:1–10), Jesus tells us that there is more joy in heaven over the return of one sinner than over ninety-nine who are just. The news gets better! Jesus is the Good Shepherd who leaves the ninety-nine and seeks us when we are lost. When he finds us, he carries us on his shoulders and rejoices. "There is joy in heaven in the presence of the angels of God over one sinner who repents."

Can you hear the Lord cry out, "My sons, my daughters, Where are you? Why do you hide from me? Let me hear your voices" (based on Genesis 3:9)? By the wounds of Christ we are forgiven and healed. Lord, with urgency we pray that your Holy Spirit will fill us, guide us, and console us. Let us not say at the end of our days: "It all happened too fast!"

The joy of Bethlehem may sometimes seem too distant from the realities of our secular world. This world does not value repentance and conversion, so the change must begin in our own hearts. The conflicts in our world are our conflicts. They involve us. Consider again the message of Jonah (3:1–10). The Lord said, "Get up, go to Nineveh, the great city, and proclaim…forty days more, and Nineveh shall be destroyed." The people of Nineveh proclaimed a great fast and put on sackcloth. Even the king sat in ashes and decreed that the animals, as well, would fast and not drink water. Then God decided to forgive them. God is sending us, too, to announce the need for prayer and fasting. God can influence world events today as well. Perhaps prayer and fasting can bring about what all the violence in the world cannot. What better time than now for repentance, for prayer, and for compassion toward those in need!

> Peace begins in our own hearts.

The greatest prayer comes from the one who repents. Picture this scene: "Dad, I did something really stupid. I'm the one who took the money from the purse. Please don't punish the other kids for what I did. I'm sorry." Picture a just and loving father's reaction: "I forgive you. Now I can use this situation to make this a better family." Our heavenly Father, too, is moved by our repentance. Through prayer and fasting great calamities—like the one in Nineveh—can be averted. Through our regular prayer, penance, and almsgiving we can turn our hearts and other hearts to God. We can reflect love and peace to our families, to our neighbors, and to our world. Peace begins in our own hearts.

### Know Your Gifts

*The story is told of a poor man who had never flown in an airplane. He had finally scraped up enough money to visit his brother in another country. On the flight he politely refused the dinner offered by the flight attendant. She asked if he wanted it later, but still he declined. After they landed, the attendant asked him why he had refused the meal. He replied that he had spent all his money on the ticket. Only then did he discover that the meal was included in the ticket.*

—*The Word Among Us*, September 2002

Do we realize that God has given us a free ticket through the death and resurrection of his Son and through the Holy Spirit? Or are we like the man on the flight who does not accept what is given to him? Rejoice in the gifts you have been given! God takes us back, time and again, and removes our shame. "I will espouse you to me for-

**With love comes forgiveness.**

ever…in love and in mercy…in fidelity" (Hosea 2:16, 22–23). God wants us to be fired into love at all times by the Holy Spirit. We have to ask ourselves: do we faithfully respond to God's invitation? Do we seek him in the community of believers he has given us? Do we seek God in Scripture and through daily prayer? We may be sinners, but we can always turn to God. We can turn and return. God is faithful, even when we are not. "My dear people, let us love one another since love comes from God….God is love….Since God has loved so much, we too should love one another…as long as we love one another God lives in us…and lets us share his Spirit" (1 John 4:7–13).

With love comes forgiveness. When it comes to remembering to forgive others, we all suffer from short-term memory loss. We are reminded daily to forgive others: "forgive us our trespasses as we forgive those who trespass against us." So why can't we forgive as we are forgiven?

## The Extent of Forgiveness

*A bitter man was walking in the woods one day. As he thought about his life, he remembered those who had lied about him and cheated him. He thought about his family that had passed on and his illness for which there was no cure. His very soul was filled with anger, resentment, and frustration. Searching for answers, he knelt at the base of an old oak tree. Tearfully he prayed: "Lord, today, you ask me to forgive; I cannot. It is not fair. I didn't deserve these wrongs done against me, and I shouldn't have to forgive. I cannot do it. I pray that you teach me to forgive."*

*As he knelt there he felt something fall onto his shoulder. He opened his eyes and saw something red on his shirt. He could not see the oak tree anymore, but only a large square piece of wood* in the ground. He raised his head and saw two feet held to the wood with a large spike through them. He raised his head more, and tears came to his eyes as he saw Jesus hanging on a cross. He saw spikes in Jesus' hands, a gash in his side, a torn and battered body, and deep thorns sunk into his head. Finally he saw the suffering and pain on Jesus' face. As their eyes met, the man's tears turned to sobs, and Jesus began to speak.

"Have you ever told a lie?"

The man answered, "Yes, Lord."

"Have you ever been given too much change and kept it?"

"Yes, Lord." And the man sobbed more and more.

"Have you ever taken something from work that wasn't yours?"

"Yes, Lord."

The man's crying became uncontrollable, and when Jesus turned his head from one side to the other, the man felt something fall on his other shoulder. He looked and saw that it was the blood of Jesus. When he looked back up, his eyes met those of Jesus, and there was a look of love the man had never seen or known before. Jesus said, "I didn't deserve this either, but I forgive you."

A man was driving in the rain with his six-year-old daughter Aspen. Suddenly she spoke, "Dad, I'm thinking of something."

"What are you thinking?" he asked.

"The rain," she began, "is like sin, and the windshield wipers are like God wiping our sins away."

After the chill bumps raced up his arms, he was able to respond. "That's really good, Aspen." How far would this little girl take this revelation? So he asked, "Do you notice how the rain keeps on coming? What does that tell you?"

Aspen didn't hesitate one moment with her answer: "We keep on sinning, and God just keeps on forgiving us."

Now is the time of forgiveness. How important is it that we forgive? Jesus tells us: "If you forgive others their failings, your heavenly Father will forgive you yours" (Matthew 6:14). And again Jesus says: "And when you stand alone in prayer, forgive whatever you have against anybody, so that your Father in heaven may forgive your failings too" (Mark 11:25).

To start their High Holy Day services, similar in purpose to our lenten season, the Jews blow a *shofar*, or ram's horn. It makes a sound that may startle the listener. In the month before the High Holy Days, a psalm is read every day. It is a "softening up" time for the soul. It is a time to get straight with God, to seek the source of salvation. What is really important in life becomes clear. We can do something similar during our lenten preparation: read Scripture every day, forgive others and ask forgiveness, say special prayers—all to soften up our souls for repentance. Lent tells us: now is the time of salvation. Of course every day is a day of preparation, a day of forgiveness and prayer. There is no season in the church calendar that is designated as a season of self-indulgence and sin!

Let me share some personal witness of literally journeying with the cross of Christ for ten years. I am part of a group that takes *The Mystery of the Passion of Christ* on the road. Among our props, which have traveled thousands of miles, are three wooden crosses. Our group has traveled to seventeen places for fifty-one performances. If we add to that the dozen or so rehearsals each year, we have lived the experience more than 270 times.

We call it a "mystery" because we are in touch with the nuances of the words and actions of the events surrounding Christ's agony, betrayal, suffering, death, and resurrection. Through the tears of the audience and cast, we experience the depth of the mystery of Christ's love. I remember a cast member whose shoulders shook as he wept during a rehearsal. Through personal exposure to the many little miracles along the way of our journey, our faith is strengthened. There is the excitement of evangelization: "You wouldn't believe it!" exclaims a cast member who has just born witness in a bar in

Winnipeg. We have visited residents in senior housing to present excerpts from the play, and that is yet another experience of mystery.

I have been "up on the cross" filling the role of Jesus during rehearsals, and there I have pondered the depth of Christ's love as he views us from that vantage point. And despite our frequent insensitivity to the ongoing sacrifice of the cross, he loves us the more. As Judas, I betray Christ over and over, seeing him scourged and crucified on the cross. There is an uncanny resemblance between the play and real life. How many times do I betray Christ through sin, only to be in touch once more with his sacrifice of love?

Christ freely chose the path of the cross in his Gethsemane agony. It was not easy, but he showed us that acceptance, suffering, and death lead to eternal reward. "This day you will be with me in Paradise" emphasizes the all-inclusive nature of Christ's love. He died for all, forgiving his tormentors and us: "Father, forgive them, they do not know what they do." The crucifix is the reminder of God's love for us. We need but gaze on it to know how much suffering our sins cause others. The cross calls us back to the love of Christ.

He is risen! Praised be Jesus Christ! Repent and believe the good news of our salvation. Now more than ever, "Blow the trumpet in Zion; sanctify a feast; call a solemn assembly; gather the people…" (Joel 2:15–16). "Now is the acceptable time; see, now is the day of salvation!" (2 Corinthians 6:2). In every season of the year let us make room in our hearts for new growth. The seed of faith will blossom with the help of the Spirit. New life is the promise of every step of our life's journey that takes us to the death and resurrection of Christ. Let us use the talents we possess. Let every day be a day of action. "The woods would be very silent if no birds sang except those that sang best," said Henry Van Dyke.

## Called to Bear Witness

Having experienced some of the joy of forgiveness, we must feel giddy as we begin to realize that God has commissioned us, much as he did the disciples at Pentecost, to announce the good news. "Everyone was amazed and unable to explain it; they asked one another what it meant. Some, however, laughed it off. 'They have been drinking too much new wine,' they said" (Acts 2:12–13). Indeed, I sometimes feel giddy as I share reflections with my readers. In an article called "Wit, Wisdom, and Evangelization" I shared the following:

- Exercise daily: walk with God.
- Most people want to serve God, but only in an advisory capacity.
- God doesn't call the qualified, but rather qualifies the called.
- Be ye fishers of men. You catch them, and God will clean them.
- Don't wait for six strong men to take you to church.
- Give God what's right, not what's left.

From the above wit and wisdom, we recognize that the Christian has a call to evangelize. We are called to share the joy that we receive in our hope as Christians. "It is unthinkable that a person should accept the word and give himself to the kingdom without becoming a person who bears witness to it and proclaims it in turn" (John Paul VI, *On Evangelization in the Modern World*, #24).

Blessed Mother Teresa defined evangelization this way: "You have Jesus in your heart and then carry him to the hearts of others." If we "walk with God" daily through Scripture and prayer, we can expect to experience the risen Lord. We will become aware of his love and have joy beyond the troubles of daily life. Like St. Paul, we will be able to declare, "I have seen the Lord" (1 Corinthians 15:8).

I am reminded of the American poet Ezra Pound who was imprisoned and declared insane for his political views in World War II. Still he found joy in working for good. In his poem "Commission" he declares:

Go in a friendly manner.
Go with an open speech.
Be eager to find new evils and new good.

It is more important to "find new good," however, than to look for wrongdoing. This is how God views us. We are all "good and loving souls who occasionally get lost" (Wayne Dyer, *The Prairie Messenger*, June 9, 2004). We tend to forget the good and loving part and focus instead on the negative in our lives and in our world. Consider the issue of peace in our world, for example. It starts with small steps within our own hearts.

I had an Ash Wednesday experience attending Mass at St. Anne's Church in Saskatoon a couple of years ago. At the moment when we usually exchange a handshake of peace, the priest shook us up a little. Instead of the customary greeting of peace to those around us, he asked us to pause and reflect on the lack of peace in our relationships. He then challenged us to decide on a lenten project bringing peace somewhere in our relationships.

## Peace Begins with Us

If there is to be peace on earth, let it begin with us. Let us look at our associations and build peace somewhere where there is discord. Let me share an example from my own life. Recently I saw a former student at a funeral Mass for her grandfather. She did the eulogy, and she did an excellent job. The history between us left something to be desired. To put it bluntly, we had had some unreconciled exchanges in our teacher-student relationship.

Right and wrong, or blame in the earlier situation was no longer important, but reconciliation was. By some grace I happened to meet her and her husband in a service station a couple of days after the funeral. I had already passed them and was heading out the door, but following an inner prompting, I approached her and expressed my condolences. I commented on what a fine job she had done and introduced myself to her husband. After a handshake of peaceful condolence she said, "Thank you," and I was on my way.

Somewhere in our lives and daily relationships there is a need for reconciliation. With prayerful openness to God, we can improve the state of "peace" in our families and in the world. We are already paving the way for that "meeting at the banquet table of the Lord" when we all sit and eat together.

I consider Johnny Cash a contemporary example of one who struggled with imperfections as he tried to serve the Lord and make peace with others. In the 1970s, I enjoyed Johnny Cash singing "the beer I had for breakfast wasn't bad, so I had one more for dessert." It was not until his death and the ensuing tributes that I realized what a profound influence Cash had on me and on the cultural milieu in which I grew up. So many of his songs had touched my youth and adult years as I grew up on the Saskatchewan prairies, and he inspired in me compassion for the less fortunate. He had a way of identifying with the underling, the dispossessed. Whether it was in the lines "a small kid cursing at a can that he was kicking," putting on his "cleanest dirty shirt" or the "lonesomeness" of the city on Sunday morning, Cash had a way of touching the sympathetic chord inside most of us. I recall, as a kid, often kicking a pebble along the pasture trail as I brought in the cows for milking.

The song that perhaps best epitomizes what he stood for was "Man in Black," which he composed after a college student asked him: "Why do you always wear black?" Cash wrote the song quickly enough to sing it on stage at that same college. In the song he says that he wears black for the poor and the beaten down, for prisoners, for the sick, the lonely old, in mourning for lives that might have been. And, he concludes, until things are once again "right" with the world, he will never wear white.

For me, this song echoes the beatitudes of Christ: "Happy the poor in spirit; theirs is the kingdom of heaven. Happy the gentle…Happy those who mourn…Happy those who hunger and thirst for what is right…Happy the merciful…Happy the pure in heart…Happy the peacemakers…Happy those who are persecuted in the cause of right" (Matthew 5:3–12).

Johnny Cash lived many of these beatitudes. He spent so much time performing in and visiting prisons ("Folsom Prison Blues") that many thought he had been an inmate. It was said that he knew the commandments because he had broken so many of them. He knew the world of drug addiction and alcoholism, but his redeeming quality was love—love of others, love of June Carter Cash, and love of his savior Jesus Christ.

There are many such models of virtue for us to imitate, and usually they are performing small acts of love "one by one."

## Where Is the Messiah?

*A group of rabbis was discussing where they might find the Messiah. One of them went to find the prophet Elijah and asked him, "Where is the Messiah?"*

*"He's at the city gate," Elijah said.*

*"What is he doing at the city gate?"*

*"He is sitting among the lepers."*

*"What is he doing among the lepers?"*

*"He is changing their bandages one by one."*

Expecially if we are at the far end of running the good race, we might ask: am I changing bandages, one by one? I speak here of the bandages of poverty, sickness, suffering, death, and the usual challenges to the spirit of joy in our lives. Do we notice the pains and sorrows of others? Do we bind their wounds?

This past Christmas I again took a lesson from the shepherds. In the Christmas narrative we read, "An angel of the Lord appeared to them…[and] said, 'Do not be afraid…I bring you news of great joy…a savior has been born to you; he is Christ the Lord'" (Luke 2:1–16). After this, when these same lowly shepherds spoke, everyone listened: "When they saw the child, they repeated what they had been told about him; and everyone who heard it was astonished at what the shepherds had to say" (Luke 2:17–18). Wow! Everyone listened to the shepherds.

*Running with Repentance*

This same message has been revealed to you and to me. Perhaps our friends and neighbors will listen with astonishment when we announce that the Messiah is changing bandages one by one.

## They Passed By

> The story is told that as the Holy Family hurried away from Bethlehem after the angel's warning that the Infant was in danger, they passed a farmer in his fields outside the city walls. It was early in the morning, just after dawn, and the farmer was sowing grain in his freshly plowed fields. He nodded as they passed. Joseph, leading the donkey carrying Mary and Jesus, smiled and raised a hand in greeting.
>
> Later that day, almost evening time, a group of Roman soldiers came marching out of Bethlehem on the same road. The soldiers called the farmer out of his field and harshly demanded, "Has a man and woman carrying a baby passed this way?"
>
> "Oh, yes," the farmer assured them. "They passed as I was sowing my grain." And half turning, he waved a hand toward his field, rich with tall grain, ripe and ready to harvest.
>
> —Catherine Fournier, "Flight into Egypt"

In reflecting on these things, I am drawn again and again to Joseph, who of the three on the journey is most like us. Grace touched Mary before her birth, Jesus' nature was Divine, but Joseph, like us, had to see, hear, and accept in faith. Even in his return from Egypt, (Matthew 2:18–24), Joseph had to follow the promptings of a dream with a great deal of faith. Like Joseph, we stand on the threshold of the eternal truth and, no matter how uneducated or unskilled we are, the Spirit will lead us to do great things.

Imagine Joseph holding the newborn baby in his arms. I picture the rough carpenter's hands almost entirely covering the tiny baby. His eyes must have misted as he saw this special miracle of love. I know the emotion of this moment, having held my firstborn in my hands and having pondered the miracle of love. Such a gift! Such a treasure! No doubt Jesus got to know what human struggle was like when he lived in Egypt for his first seven years, and having known our nature as a child, he fulfilled it and knew it as a man. And Joseph guided him. Joseph knew our nature, our hungers, wants, and desires. With faith like his, we can continue to trust that the Spirit will turn our simple tasks of life into great ones.

I recently read a quote by clinical counselor Joan Groff that summarizes how I see Joseph and how I would like my life to be.

"So many of us hunger for meaning in our lives and search for who God is amidst the turmoil and stress of daily living. But how often do we take time to reflect on how we perceive God is working in our everyday lives? Anyone...who takes time for this reflection will be richly rewarded" (*Theological Reflections: Finding God in Our Experiences*). She goes on to say that when we do this reflection and share our insights, we are open to change, and thus become open to transforming our lives, as Joseph did.

I would like to conclude this chapter with a reflection on St. Joseph, who was most certainly a model of virtue and faith. I picture Joseph, first in his journey to Bethlehem, and later in his flight to Egypt, to be on the threshold of Grace, like us, struggling to believe in the revelation of angels in dreams. Reality was as harsh as the Egyptian desert, and Joseph, like us, saw but through a glass darkly. But his patience and his faith led him to use the gift of his carpenter's hands to provide for Mary and Jesus the best he could. Mary pondered the mysteries of God's plan and prayerfully accepted her role in the divine plan. Much is written about their difficult journey into Egypt. Like the journeys of our lives, it was a journey of grace and special providence.

St. Alphonse Liguori speculated about this journey into Egypt, a tough journey of three hundred miles that took more than thirty days. The season was winter and there was rain and wind. Mary was fifteen. Where did they sleep? What did they eat? Two hundred miles of desert had to be traversed where robbers and wild beasts abounded. Alphonse continues to describe the seven years spent in Egypt when the family must have struggled to earn a living, having started with nothing but the rough bare hands of a carpenter. Jesus' first years were an experience of hard living, of doing without.

## For Your Reflection

*There is joy in heaven in the presence of the angels of God over one sinner who repents. (Luke 15:1–10)*
- How does this make you feel?
- As you continue your run toward God, are you in need of repentance?

*I will espouse you to me forever in love, and mercy, and fidelity. (Hosea 2:16, 22–23)*
- Imagine for a few minutes that God is speaking these words to you.
- How do you experience God's love, mercy, and fidelity at this point in your life?

*Now is the acceptable time. See, now is the day of salvation. (2 Corinthians 6:2)*
- What "time" is it for you, spiritually speaking?
- What does "day of salvation" mean for you?

*Do not be afraid. I bring you good news of great joy! (Luke 2:1–16)*
- Are you afraid in any way to be part of God's plan?
- In what ways might you bring good news to others?

# Chapter 6

# The Road All Runners Come

> Today, the road all runners come,
> Shoulder-high we bring you home.
>
> —*from "To an Athlete Dying Young" by A.E. Housman*

There is little good humor about dying, and our sensitivity to the somber nature of the process is well placed. I do recall one joke told by a priest at a funeral. The story is told of a man applying for an acting job. He had played bit parts and recited these, but he had one serious claim to fame. He had once enacted "death" and had done such a fine job that one member of the audience actually fainted. When asked, "Who was the person who fainted?" the aspiring actor replied, "My life insurance agent."

## Another Touch of Humor

> An elderly woman died last month. Having never married, she requested no male pallbearers. In her handwritten instructions for her memorial service, she wrote, "They wouldn't take me

*out while I was alive, I don't want them to take me out when I'm dead."*

Housman's line at the start of this chapter, "the road all runners come," conjures up various images for me: Christ walking toward Jerusalem, a loved one diagnosed with cancer, and the slowly debilitating process of aging. What makes these bearable is that Jesus is central to our journey and is vitally interested in us every step of the way. I wonder sometimes what Jesus might say to us about this road we must all travel. Here's what I think he would say:

> *All suffering can be united to the suffering of Christ's cross.*

I love you. You have hardships and suffering in your lives.

I want to make it better for you. I want to ease your suffering.

Know that suffering leads to resurrection and eternal joy.

Know that when you face sickness and death I am with you.

You are not alone. I too have suffered and died.

I have won the victory over death.

In a short time you will be with me and I will serve you at my Father's table.

In the meantime, I leave with you my Body and Blood, food for your mind and spirit.

Receive my bread and let it strengthen you for your journey.

Another way of glimpsing our mortality is presented in the words of the song, "O Land of Rest" (We'll Work till Jesus Comes). Here the emphasis is on continuing to serve and work hard until the Lord comes at the time of our death. In Catholic hymnals this song is called "Jerusalem My Happy Home." The lyrics here are about reaching the place where there is no more sorrow, no more sickness, but life forevermore among the saints.

O land of rest, for thee I sigh!
When will the moment come
When I shall lay my armor by
And dwell in peace at home?

We'll work till Jesus comes
We'll work till Jesus comes
We'll work till Jesus comes
And we'll be gathered home
To Jesus Christ I fled for rest
He bade me cease to roam
And lean for comfort on His breast
Till He conduct me home

I sought at once my Savior's side
No more my steps shall roam
With Him I'll brave death's chilling tide
And reach my heav'nly home

## Denying Our Mortality

In this life we are not normally concerned about the immediacy of the "New Jerusalem" and all it implies. Our concern is mostly for the here and now. We spend years denying our mortality. The consoling thought as we leave the church after a funeral is the secret knowledge that we are right again; that death is something that happens to other people. We live in a culture that denies death. Many of us do question the meaning of death especially when disasters strike. We ask: how can God allow such things to happen? Why does God allow wars and natural disasters to take so many innocent lives? Both death and suffering are mysteries, related to the Paschal mystery. Simply: Jesus suffered and died to redeem us. His glorious resurrection and our hope of rising are the fruit of that sacrifice. All suffering can be united to the suffering of Christ's cross and participate in that action of salvation. In this sense all suffering has deep meaning. God's love is an unquestioned constant, but so is suffering and death in our world. Mary, the mother of Jesus, suffered particular sorrows. Jesus, God's son, suffered immeasurable pain and a most cruel death. The promise Jesus gave us is, "I am the way and the truth and the life" (John 14:6). We all go to the Father through Jesus. The "way" will include death and suffering in this world.

I like to add the perspective of "time" to death. In the following story, it's done with a touch of humor.

### A Good Long Life

*Three Irishmen, Paddy, Sean, and Seamus, were stumbling home from the pub late one night and found themselves on the road that led past the old graveyard.*

*"Come have a look over here," said Paddy. "It's Michael O'Grady's grave, God bless his soul. He lived to the ripe old age of eighty-seven."*

*"That's nothing," said Sean. "Here's one named Patrick O'Toole; it says here that he was ninety-five when he died!"*

*Just then, Seamus yelled out, "Good God, here's a fella that got to be 145!"*

*"What was his name?" asked Paddy.*

*Seamus stumbled around a bit, awkwardly lights a match to see what else is written on the stone marker, and exclaimed, "Miles from Dublin."*

One thousand years from now the particulars about how we died, whether from illness, accident, war, or disease will be insignificant. What will be significant is that Jesus was "the way, the truth and the life," and that we followed him. Then we will be able to see the love that is God. We will be in that place where there are no tears, where all are equal and blessed.

To every thing there is a season. There is a time for every purpose under heaven: "a time for giving birth, a time for dying…a time for tears…a time for laughter. A time for embracing, a time to refrain from embracing…a time for keeping silent, a time for speaking" (Ecclesiastes 3:1–8).

Two years ago, I was visiting my brother-in-law in the hospital. He had just suffered a heart attack, and I realized he was experiencing a "season of the soul." I took note of the date for another reason as well. In another bed of the same ward, also in for treatment, was the man I mentioned earlier, the oldest survivor of the holocaust. As I watched him facing east, wearing his yarmulke and Tallit and saying his prayers, I realized that I was witness to a special moment of grace. In his presence, I realized in a profound way that the human spirit is indeed alive and well. How many times has this man been in touch with his God, shared his Lord's wisdom, and contemplated God's plan for him? I was in awe of my brother-in-law's presence as well—for another reason. Let me explain.

*To every thing there is a season.*

The morning of his angiogram, after implanting a stint to open a blocked passageway, my brother-in-law was in a deep rest when I entered the room. I stood in silence and observed him for a moment. I was struck by his absolute resemblance to Jesus Christ. I pondered for a moment about how we can see Christ in others, but that did not explain why I was seeing Jesus Christ before me. Later I reasoned that his long hair and beard were a factor, but it took a while for me to again see only my brother-in-law. There was something Christ-like about his accepting this sudden radical turn in his life. There was no complaint about the heart attack. There was no complaint about pain—in fact the angiogram procedure was done later than planned and the anesthetic had all but worn off so that he felt practically everything in silent acceptance. Perhaps my brother-in-law had accepted all of the suffering of his condition and offered it up in prayer. It was certainly not easy to change from being a strong, healthy, working man one day to a convalescing heart patient the next. His life, and in a sense his soul, had entered a new season. This day I felt assured that he was an instrument of the Lord.

The Book of Wisdom offers us this insight and hope about the debilitating changes that all of us will one day face: "If they experienced punishment [suffering], their hope was rich with immortality; slight was their affliction, great will their blessings be. God has put them to the test and proved them worthy to be with him; he has tested them like gold in a furnace, and accepted them as a holocaust... (We all look forward to the day of our reward in heaven, in the next life.) When the time comes for his visitation they will shine out; as sparks run through stubble, so will they. They shall judge nations, rule over peoples...grace and mercy await those he has chosen" (Wisdom 3:4–9).

When it comes to understanding suffering there is one group that gives us examples of endurance and adds to the richness of our world—our seniors.

## How Old?

*A little girl asks her mother, "How old is Grandma?"*
*"She's twenty-nine and holding," the wise mother replies.*
*"Well," asks the little girl, "how old would she be if she let go?"*

I hope Grandma can "hold on" a little longer. We have so much to learn from her.

Children can see the richness of old age far better than we sometimes can. Consider the poem "Walking with Grandpa":

I like to walk with Grandpa;
    His steps are short like mine.
He doesn't say "Hurry up."
    He always takes his time.
I like to walk with Grandpa;
    His eyes see things like mine do:
Wee pebbles bright, and a funny cloud,
    Half-hidden drops of dew.
Most people have to hurry;
    They do not stop and see.

> I'm glad that God made Grandpa
> Unrushed and young like me.
>
> —Author Unknown

Our seniors are blessed with what truly matters. They embody so much knowledge, so much experience, so much realization, and so much truth. A senior's home is a special branch of the Communion of Saints. We know that suffering entered the world through sin. We know that Jesus broke the power of sin and took the suffering that was our due. "By his stripes we were healed." Jesus is God's gift of love to us every day. In the lives of our seniors, we see the patient endurance of suffering in our human condition, which often involves sickness, sadness, and death. Most of us would not choose such a state voluntarily. This condition is temporary, but the crown of reward is eternal.

Our seniors are a sign to us. Their often-silent acceptance of a state of health that we naturally balk at gives them a share in the redemptive suffering of Christ. They are a sign to us of the suffering and punishment that, except for the sacrifice of Christ, normally is our due because of our sins. They are also a reminder of the great gift of Christ who took all this suffering on himself and offered it up to the Father as atonement for us. The seniors, in their turn, partake of this suffering of Christ for the redemption of all. Their suffering is Christ's suffering. Through their actions and very existence they make the world richer, especially their little corner of it. There is so much to learn from the journey our seniors are making before us.

## What Is True Beauty?

*Once upon a time there was a magic mirror on the wall. An elder approached the mirror and asked, "Mirror, mirror, on the wall, who is the fairest of them all?"*

*The mirror replied, "Many in the land of youth are supple and suave, but your beauty far surpasses all of these."*

*"How can that be?" asked the senior.*

*"I am a magic mirror," replied the reflector, "and just as the still water reflects the beauty of the flowers and trees that grow along its banks, I echo what is true and becoming."*

*"But I have blotches on my skin of which I have too much for my frame. Many say I am old and ugly."*

*"I am a mirror of the soul. Learn this truth: love transforms whatever is imperfect into beauty. Beauty is truth and truth is beauty."*

As a child I remember reading a poem by Leigh Hunt called "Abou Ben Adhem." In this fable, a tribal leader had a vision of an angel who was writing names in a golden book.

"What writest thou?" Abou asked.

"The names of those who love the Lord," replied the vision.

"Write me as one that loves his fellow man," Abou said.

The next night the angel reappeared and shared the names of those whom "love of God had pleased, and lo! Ben Adhem's name led all the rest!"

Truly what counts for beauty before God is how we love others. The most beautiful people I know on this earth are those who are a blessing to everyone around them. I have a friend in a senior's home who literally "blesses" all who serve her. Her short litany of words concludes with, "…that God may give you health and strength for many, many years to come." I have long since concluded that the blessings she imparts must refer to the place of beauty and joy we call heaven. Here on earth we physically get older and feebler with each passing year.

God is the final judge of what is beautiful. The more truth and love grow in us, the more beautiful, the more Christ-like, we become. In the misplaced values of this world, beauty is often confused with youth. That kind of beauty fades. We need to frequently check our images in the mirror of the soul. From year to year we should be progressing in the love of the Lord. Some of the most beautiful people I know never grew old. My mother and father didn't get old, but they got beautiful.

When I look at the printed word, even the word of God, I cannot read it without my glasses. The small letters are a blur. This is a result of being farsighted and getting older. For most of my life I didn't need reading glasses. Spiritually the opposite is true. I can see things very clearly now that were a blur to me in my youth. Especially is this true when I look at the word of God. In Isaiah 55:10–11, the Lord tells us that his word that is proclaimed will not return to him empty, but it will accomplish the purpose for which he sent it. To make it still easier for us to grasp, the Word becomes flesh in Jesus.

> The more truth and love grow in us, the more Christ-like we become.

The message of John 3:17 tells us God sent his son not to condemn the world but to save it. And in a dramatic fashion Jesus announces that he is the Messiah Isaiah spoke of: "The spirit of the Lord has been given to me...He has sent me to bring the good news to the poor, to proclaim liberty to captives and to the blind new sight, to set the down-trodden free" (Luke 4:18).

We are at a special moment in time. Until now "the whole of creation has been groaning in labor pains" (Romans 8:23), waiting for this time of salvation. Blessed are our eyes to see what we see and our ears to hear what we hear (Matthew 13:16). Truly, there is immediacy to the opportunities of today. For this we were born and all our days have led us to this moment and this time to choose.

Yes, as we grow older our optical vision becomes impaired, but our spiritual sight becomes clearer. We have assurances from our maker that when our eyesight fails completely and our journey on this earth is at an end, then our eternal vision will be at its brightest.

Recently when I visited the seniors' lodge in Canora I was led to ponder, "What would Jesus see if he visited this place?" Now I realize that he frequents homes like this one. When we look closely, we see faith that abides; we see hope even where our worldly eyes are blind; and we see love that endures.

Wherever we are on life's continuum, we can gain much wisdom reflecting on the life, suffering, and death of Jesus Christ. In daily prayer moments, in the quiet of our hearts, we need to let Jesus teach us, love us, and show us what he has in store for us. The Lord "…is found by those who do not put him to the test, and manifests himself to those who do not distrust him" (Wisdom 1:2).

## Through a Glass Darkly

Our understanding of the hereafter is now, at best, seen by us as through a glass darkly (1 Corinthians 13:11–12). Then we shall see the truth as it is. One of the best ways to study the hope of eternal life is through reflecting on Easter and its mysteries. Easter is the antidote to death. Death has its origin in sin, and a way to combat death is by living a life that becomes increasingly removed from sin.

The miracle of Easter is not something from the distant past; it is something we need to understand today. The resurrection is still happening, and the sacrifice of Christ is ongoing to bring forgiveness and conversion to all. With our eyes opened and our ears awakened, we can grasp the miracle of Easter—like Edith Burns in the story that follows.

> *Edith would introduce herself to anyone and everyone saying, "Hello, my name is Edith Burns. Do you believe in Easter?" Then she would explain the Easter story.*
>
> *One day her doctor had bad news. Edith had cancer and not long to live.*
>
> *Edith said, "You have told me I'm going to see my precious Lord Jesus and celebrate Easter forever, and you're sad?"*

*The head nurse, Phyllis Cross, was not sold on the Easter story and told Edith, "You can quit praying for me, it won't work."*

"Then I will ask God not to let me go home until you come into the family," Edith said. The battle was engaged until one day Phyllis was drawn to Edith's room.

Edith greeted her, "I'm so glad you came, because God told me that today is your special day."

"Edith, you have asked everybody else. 'Do you believe in Easter?' but you have never asked me."

"God told me to wait until you asked. Do you believe that Jesus is alive and that he wants to live in your heart?"

"I want to believe that with all my heart, and I do want Jesus in my life." Phyllis said. Her heart was suddenly lifted and she practically floated out of the room.

On Easter Sunday when Phyllis came to bring Easter lilies and to wish Edith a Happy Easter, Edith's hands were in the Bible. A sweet smile was on her face. But Edith was dead. Her left hand was on John 14, "In my Father's house are many mansions. I go to prepare a place for you." Her right hand was on Revelation 21:4, "And God will wipe away every tear from their eyes, there shall be no more death, nor sorrow, nor crying, and there shall be no more pain, for former things have passed away."

As Phyllis left the room she met two student nurses.

She said, "My name is Phyllis Cross. Do you believe in Easter?"

Many of our forebears saw the star of faith and followed it. Many lived with the vision of faith. I have personally seen this and have heard others witness about it. Shortly before her death, my mother seemed to raise her head from her pillow and fix her eyes on something in the room, which we could not see. She broke into a beautiful smile. My wife witnessed the same event with her father's passing. St. Stephen, as he was being stoned to death for his faith, said, "I see the heavens opened and the Son of Man standing at the right hand of God" (Acts 7:56). Imagine the thoughts of John the Baptist, just before his execution. These two examples should inspire us to celebrate Christianity and proclaim it. Imagine the thoughts of Jesus on the cross when evil seemed to be triumphing and his supporters had fled. Even then, Jesus said, "Father, into your hands I commend my Spirit."

It is inspiring to know that the Holy Spirit of grace is at work in us, and whatever good we set in motion in our brief lives will continue to bear fruit even after we are gone, just as it did for John the Baptist and for Christ. These thoughts are but a small part of the inspiration we gain from reflecting on the passion of Jesus and its influence on the lives of the saints. Suffering is something we generally don't do well and try to avoid. But Jesus Christ embraced it with a passion.

Meditating on the Passion of Christ can bear much spiritual fruit. St. Augustine writes that, "There is no more profitable occupation for the soul than to meditate daily on the Passion of Our Lord." St. Alphonse says that all the saints became saints by devotion to the Passion and that there was no saint who did not have a great love of the Passion. The venerable Anne Catherine Emmerich, a German Augustinian nun, bore the sacred stigmata (the wounds of Christ and the crown of thorns). During the last twelve years of her life she ate no food except for Holy Communion. She saw many visions, detailed in a book *The Dolorous Passion of Our Lord Jesus Christ*, about the sufferings of our Lord. Mel Gibson used this source in preparing the movie *The Passion of the Christ*.

How does the reality of the Passion of Christ impact our lives? We all grapple with sin in our lives. The inevitability of death looms somewhere in our future. Perhaps like Christ we need a transfiguration (Matthew 17:1–9) to prepare us for that trip to Calvary. We continue to live in faith and hope, knowing that suffering and death are a part of our spiritual history. But thanks be to God, we also live with the knowledge of redemption through the ongoing work of Christ. My own father's death was such a participation in the ongoing work of Christ, and is a rich legacy to me. He died of cancer and struggled against it to his last breath. On his last day, I rushed to his bedside, the words of Dylan Thomas echoing in my mind: "Do not go gentle into that good night."

## The Human Struggle

My father's struggle was a blessed realization to me. It is nature's way to struggle for breath as long as possible. I remember my father's last breath, and the victory that I saw in his wasted body. He looked like a king in that moment, the image of a "finished Christ." I knew that he had fought the good fight. I knew that his spirit was greater than his body and had survived. I stepped out of the hospital into the December night and I looked heavenward through the streaming snowflakes to see if I could discern the path of his spirit's flight. One of my most treasured moments was to be present at my father's death, to see a good man die.

Poets and mystics through the centuries have passed on a rich legacy about the struggle of the human spirit "not unbecoming men that strove with gods"(Tennyson). The Graveyard Poets of the seventeenth century compared this life to a time of waiting for the light and the life of the next world: "Live ever in the womb, not see the light?" and "When shall I die, when shall I live forever?" Thomas Gray in his "Elegy" tried to "teach the rustic moralist to die" (84).

Shakespeare's Caesar said:

Of all the wonders that I have heard,
It seems to me most strange that men should fear;
Seeing that death, a necessary end,
Will come when it will come (II. ii. 34–37).

Let's look now for a moment at the Christian perspective regarding death. For the Christian with deep faith, the words of Jesus explain it clearly: "I solemnly assure you, those who hear my word and have faith in him who sent me possess eternal life. They do not come under damnation, but have passed from death to life" (John 5:24).

Fundamental to finding joy in dying is the belief in a better life after this one. The question of how to prepare for the next life is faced in various ways by the different world religions. Hinduism teaches that the soul never dies, but is reincarnated until a state of spiritual perfection is reached. Hindu faith believes in worshiping some who have died and are saints. This parallels the Christian belief in a Communion of Saints that includes the living and the deceased, who can be a good influence on us. Buddhism believes in reincarnation until Nirvana is achieved. A teaching of Buddhism is that on earth you are never completely free of suffering and pain, but the upside is that this world prepares you for a better position in the next, until you are freed from the wheel of life.

One aspect of preparation for death that runs like a common theme through these religions is repentance. In "The Hollow Men," T.S. Eliot reflects on the unpreparedness of those without faith facing death, and he says that life ends "not with a bang, but a whimper." Our lives should lead us to repentance for our human failings, our deliberate sins. "Repent and believe the good news," the good news that Christ has overcome death for us. Christ died for all the sins of mankind. As we contemplate death, this is the greatest secret for peaceful and happy acceptance. His act of love was great enough to redeem even us.

A clear example that gives us great consolation and hope is that of the thief on the cross next to Christ. Most of us could compare our lives and our record favorably with that of this brigand who said to Christ: "Remember me when you come into your kingdom." Jesus was very explicit in rewarding this man's simple act of faith: "This day you will be with me in Paradise."

Saints and martyrs have gone joyfully to their deaths. If we look beyond the apparent fanaticism this implies, we see the simple yet absolute faith that not only made happiness in death a possibility, but also made happiness in this life a reality.

As we plot the course of our lives, most of us choose a path somewhere between the uncontrolled indulgences of human desires, on the one extreme, and the rigid self-denial and penance of an ascetic religious quest. This sounds much like the "Middle Way" of the Buddhist. We must avoid living our lives always at the mercy of some self-serving passion or indulgence, which is more slavery than freedom. Happiness comes from giving to and receiving from others. The joy of love begins in this world but finds its fulfillment in the hereafter.

> The joy of love begins in this world but finds its fulfillment in the hereafter.

## What Will Death Be Like?

Another ultimate question we face as our lives draw toward an end is: what will death be like? Before my father died he asked this question of my priest brother. This question puzzled me. I thought my dad had always known the answer. He said death is like falling asleep and awakening the next morning—a continuation of the best love of this life. Our deceased relatives and friends will be there to greet us. I think what my father was experiencing at the moment of his question was a natural fear of the unknown. It was a human confession such as Christ made the night before his death when he cried out to the Father to take "this cup" away from him. And later, as he hung on the cross, he cried out, "My God! My God! Why have you forsaken me?"

The joy of dying can be experienced by simple folks as well as saints. Recently an eighty-one-year-old aunt of mine died. She had been a member of a large family, and all but one had passed away. When I heard the news, I celebrated briefly with my family by bringing out the Christmas candy early. My teenage son said, "Dad, you have a strange way of looking at things." I explained that my aunt had recently said that she wouldn't mind falling asleep and not waking up in the morning. She was ready to die. She said, "When you reach the point where there is more waiting for you on the other side than in this world, it's time to die." She got her wish, and so we celebrated.

In conclusion I would like to address the sadness and pain of the final farewell that seems to wrench all joy from our experience of death. We need to balance the sadness of "departure" with the real joy of "arrival" of the one in the eternal realm where surely relatives and friends already there echo the glad shout, "Here she comes!"

> *I am standing upon the seashore. A ship at my side spreads her white sails to the morning breeze and starts for the blue ocean. She is an object of beauty and strength, and I stand and watch until at last she hangs like a speck of white cloud just where the sun and sky come down to mingle with each other. Then someone at my side says, "There she goes!"*
>
> *Gone where? Gone from my sight—that is all. She is just as large in mast and hull and spar as she was when she left my side and just as able to bear her load of living freight to the place of her destination.*
>
> *Her diminished size is in me, not in her. And just at the moment when someone at my side says, "There she goes!" there are other eyes watching her coming and other voices ready to take up the glad shout, "Here she comes!"*
>
> —Henry van Dyke's "A Parable of Immortality"

To every thing there is a season, and a time to every purpose under heaven…a time to be born, a time to die.

 For Your Reflection

*I am the Way and the Truth and the Life. (John 14:6)*
- How do you feel about these words of Jesus?
- What comfort do they give you as you "run the good race"?

*God has put them to the test and proved them worthy.*
*(Wisdom 3:4–9)*
- What "test" have you been put through in recent years?
- How does it feel to know that God has proved you worthy?

*For now we see through a glass darkly; but then face to face.*
*(1 Corinthians 13:12)*
- When you ponder "eternal life," what images come to you?
- Do you ever think about seeing God "face to face"?

*And God will wipe away every tear from their eyes; there shall be no more death, nor sorrow, nor crying, and there shall be no more pain, for former things have passed away.*
*(Revelation 21:4).*
- Spend time today reflecting on this beautiful description of how life will be when you die.
- Do you believe in Easter?

Chapter 7

# Running to See God

Speak now to God and say in your whole heart:
"I seek your face. Your face, Lord, I desire."

—*St. Anselm*

*The true story is told of a priest who was killed in a car accident. He was following a snowplow during a storm, turned out to pass and hit a semi head on. As another priest put it, "He met Jesus face to face." Some would say, "That was a terrible way to meet Jesus"; others might say, "It's always great to meet Jesus face to face."*

St. Anselm describes how we can meet Jesus face to face: "Escape from everyday business for a short while…make a little time for God and rest a little in him. Enter into your mind's inner chamber. Shut out everything but God. In 1 Corinthians 13:12, St. Paul says: "For now we see in a mirror, dimly, but then we will see face to face. Now I know only in part; then I will know fully." Have you seen or recognized Jesus lately? More importantly, have you been Jesus to someone lately?

I was privileged recently to participate in a "Face to Face" weekend retreat for youth and adults. The facilitator did a Spirit-filled job of leading young people (and us) to an encounter with the Lord. In praise, in song, and in silent adoration we came before the Lord to touch his face, to bask in his presence. Old hurts were healed, old wrongs forgiven, and the Eucharist was shared.

## How Do We Meet Jesus?

One question that inspired and moved us during this weekend is a favorite of mine: how do we meet Jesus in our day-to-day encounters? In my book *Where Earth Meets Heaven* I shared a story about ancient monks who traveled the earth in search of the place where earth meets heaven. Finally one day they found a door that marked the spot. When they opened it and stepped through, they found themselves back in their monastery where they lived their daily lives. This is the place where we meet or miss the Lord. The impact of this story and the success of its lesson were brought home to me by a reader from Winnipeg who was excited about sharing the following with me. He had been watching a grandfather assisting his grandchildren all day, driving this one to a hockey practice, that one to another event. After observing the love and devotion of this grandparent it struck him: this is where earth meets heaven.

Some of the tenets of the "Face to Face" retreat can be used by all of us. They include

1. Win: to win people to Jesus by proclaiming the personal love of God;

2. Build: to personally build a knowledge of our Christian faith;

3. Send: to be sent out to spread the kingdom of God through word and deed.

Through baptism we are anointed prophet, priest, and king. We are brothers and sisters of Christ and heirs of the royal kingdom. We are royalty! And we are commissioned to go forth and proclaim the good news of Christ's kingdom. After encountering God face to face, we go forth "through him, with him and in him" to a world that is starving for good news. Like the apostles, we are weak and sometimes foolish sinners, but Jesus calls us to be a "work in progress," to cooperate with grace, and to be with him in prayer so that the Holy Spirit can lead us to be a blessing to those around us.

In this chapter, we will explore several aspects of meeting God face to face through prayer.

## Doing Your Part

Most of you have heard the story of the man who kept asking God, "Please God, let me win the lottery."

After much pleading, God finally says to the man, "Could you at least buy a ticket?"

We do not always appear to get our prayers answered.

## God Answers Unselfish Prayer

*There was a shipwreck and two survivors swam to a small, deserted island. They agreed to pray for help. To find out whose prayer was more powerful, they stayed on opposite sides of the island.*

*First they prayed for food. Next morning, the first person saw a fruit tree on his side of the island, but his buddy had nothing. In turn the first man prayed for a wife, a house, clothes, and more food. All of these appeared while his buddy had nothing. Finally, the first man prayed for a ship. When a ship appeared, he decided to leave his buddy on the island, since God had not answered any of his prayers.*

*As he was leaving, a voice from heaven boomed, "Why are you leaving your companion on the island?"*

*"My blessings are mine, since I prayed for them. His prayers were unanswered, and he deserves nothing."*

*"You are mistaken!" the voice rebuked. "He had only one prayer, which I answered. He prayed that all your prayers be answered."*

Whether we pray for our own needs or the needs of others, how confident are we when we pray? I would like always to pray with the trust of blind Bartimaeus as he throws off his coat (security blanket) and moves toward Jesus (Mark 10:46). In Mark 9:19, Jesus expresses frustration with his disciples who could not cure an epileptic demoniac: "You faithless generation…how much longer must I be with you?" Yet he assures them, "Everything is possible for anyone who has faith." With faith we can move mountains. In Mark 11:23–24, Jesus says: "I tell you solemnly, if anyone says to this mountain, 'Get up and throw yourself into the sea,' with no hesitation, it will be done. I tell you therefore: everything you ask for, believe that you have it already, and it will be yours."

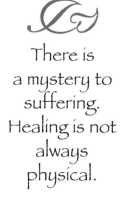

There is a mystery to suffering. Healing is not always physical.

## Ask Repeatedly

Most of us know what we want when we pray. Scripture tells us we need to ask and ask and ask. In fact, when asked by one of his disciples: "Lord teach us to pray" (Luke 11:1), Jesus gave us a prayer we can say daily, asking for our bread, forgiveness, and a life of grace. The Lord's Prayer also prays for the world, for God's kingdom to come. It is certainly worth praying daily and reflecting on the various aspects of this prayer. But why do we so often feel our prayers are not answered? What can we say to those who pray and are not healed?

Certainly there is a mystery to suffering. Healing is not always physical. God asks some to carry a cross of sickness and some to endure other suffering. All are loved. That is the one thing we can be sure of. I have often puzzled about God the Father's reaction or response to the prayers of his son Jesus in Gethsemane and on the cross: "Let this cup pass….My God, My God, why have you forsaken me?" The cup of suffering was not removed. The prayer seemed unanswered. The Father looked on, but surely he was not indifferent.

The greater glory of the resurrection prevailed. The world was redeemed, but at a tremendous cost, with a tremendous love. The physical signs tell us what happened. The temple veil was torn in two. The earth shook. Heaven was opened and love and forgiveness ensued. It began even before the death of Jesus as he forgave the cohort crucifying him and promised the thief on his right that he would be in heaven with him. Sometimes our prayers seem unanswered and God seems distant. But the truth is that we have in Jesus one who understands human suffering. We pray to one who has suffered and died. Somehow it is easier to relate to such love.

I am reminded of the amusing anecdote (below) about the power of Scripture.

### Stopped in His Tracks

*An elderly woman had just returned to her home from an evening of Church services when she was startled by an intruder. She caught the man in the act of robbing her home of its valuables and yelled, "Stop! Acts 2:38!" ("Repent and be baptized, in the name of Jesus Christ so that your sins may be forgiven.") The burglar stopped in his tracks. The woman calmly called the police and explained what she had done.*

*As the officer cuffed the man to take him in, he asked the burglar, "Why did you just stand there? All the old lady did was yell a Scripture passage to you."*

*"Scripture?" replied the burglar. "She said she had an Ax and two 38s!"*

In reality, our experience of Scripture is not so dramatic or humorous. But do not be mistaken! God's word has the power to change lives. Let me illustrate: imagine a young man and woman deeply in love. Every date is exciting, every encounter breathtaking. The power of such love has inspired poets and songwriters for centuries. Imagine the same couple after eating forty thousand meals together. Unless they have cultivated and nurtured their love, they can only dream about the love that once was.

Our love affair with God has to be nurtured as well. As children we perhaps were very close to God. Faith was as simple as mommy and daddy's love for us. We knew God loved us just as much because they said so. Over the years, especially in the teen years, we perhaps got more distant from that love and even questioned it—just as we questioned the authority (and sometimes love) of our parents.

Just as in the example of the lovers spending forty years together, our love affair with God needs to be nurtured and cultivated. Perhaps the best way is through love letters. God has sent us love letters in the sands of time. One of my favorites is the book of Hosea 11:1–4. "Hear the word of the Lord, O people. 'When Israel was a child, I loved him, out of Egypt I called my son. The more I called them, the more they went from us.'"

Isn't that you and me? As children, God called us. As we grew older, the more God called, the more we "went from" him. The passage continues: "Yet it was I who taught Ephraim to walk; I took them up in my arms; but they did not know that I healed them [how often the Lord delivers us from danger, from an accidental death]. I led them with cords of human kindness, with bonds of love." Through our parents, God continued to love us: "I was to them like those who lift infants to cheek. I bent to them and fed them."

## Re-read the Letters

If we have grown "cool" to the love of God for us, we need to pick up God's word and read again some of these love letters. Perhaps we need to start "dating" again, to meet and make time for our lover. We need to ponder, to reflect on God's great love for us. Realization comes through contemplation! Reflecting on God's love will give us hope and a fresh start.

Spring is the season of nature that renews our hope with the budding of new life and the signs of new growth. The meadowlark tells our hearts that once again a new grace may reveal new hope and fill our hearts with joy. Once again we know it is possible to see God face to face.

Just as resurrection for Jesus could only come about after the agony of the cross and the crucifixion on Calvary, in our lives, too, there are daily crosses that will lead to resurrection. We can carry them with joy if we put our faith in Christ, and try to see God through his eyes.

## Christ, Our Morning Star

Find some time in the next few days to reflect on these words from the Easter Vigil's "Exultet," which offer us the promise of resurrection.

> May the power of that holy night dispel all evil,
> wash guilt away, restore lost innocence,
> bring mourners joy, cast out hatred,
> bring us peace, and humble earthly pride.
> May the Morning Star which never sets
> find this flame [of Easter light] still burning:
> Christ, that Morning Star, who came back from the dead,
> and shed his peaceful light on all the earth.

Sometimes we don't see the results of our prayer, but when we pray "in Christ," we believe that God hears us. Jesus did not leave us empty-handed before returning to the Father. In fact, he came back to make sure we understand. His journey with the two disciples on the way to Emmaus gives us a detailed lesson of what is the most important aspect of our relationship with him and the Father. We are those disciples when we pray: "Stay with us Lord, as we journey with you and the disciples on the road to Emmaus (Luke 24). As you walk with us, explain to us the passages throughout Scripture that are about you. It is getting late, so stay with us.

Join us at table and say the blessing and break bread with us that our eyes might be opened!"

Jesus said, "I am the living bread which has come down from heaven. Anyone who eats this bread will live forever; and the bread that I shall give is my flesh, for the life of the world" (John 6:51).

The Scripture then says that this shocked the Jews. How could he give them his flesh to eat? He answered by saying, "I tell you most solemnly, if you do not eat the flesh of the Son of Man and drink his blood, you will not have life in you. Anyone who does eat my flesh and drink my blood has eternal life, and I shall raise him up on the last day" (John 6:53–59). These were very powerful words, and they are the words of Jesus Christ! He was telling them that the bread that he would give for the life of the world was his flesh.

The Eucharist is a memorial celebration that points to future events: "…do this in memory of me" (Luke 22:19). We proclaim the death and resurrection of Jesus and we look to his future coming, though believing that Jesus is, in fact, still with us. "I am with you always" (Matthew 28:20). We recognize Jesus' presence in the Word made flesh and his presence among us "when two or more are gathered" in his name (Matthew 18:20).

The Eucharist is a meal that demands unity. In the "priestly" prayer with his disciples at the Last Supper Jesus prays: "May they all be one. Father, may they be one in us, as you are in me and I am in you, so that the world may believe it was you who sent me" (John 17:21–23). St. Paul echoes this theme and challenges us first in 1 Corinthians 10:17 when he says: "The fact that there is only one loaf means that, though there are many of us, we form a single body because we all have a share in this one loaf." Then later in Ephesians 4:4 he says: "There is one Body, one Spirit, just as you were all called into one and the same hope when you were called. There is one Lord, one faith, one baptism, and one God who is Father of all, over all, through all and within all."

Stay with us Lord! Help us recognize you in the breaking of bread. Help us to set out immediately (Luke 24:33) while our hearts burn within us. As we contemplate the mystery of the Eucharist and reverence its presence among us, may we become one in the Lord and united with one another. It is above all the Eucharist that sustains us as we head toward meeting God face to face.

 ## For Your Reflection

*Ask and it will be given to you. (Matthew 7:7)*
- What do you ask of God right now, at this very moment?
- What are your deepest needs?

*Everything is possible for one who has faith. (Mark 9:19)*
- How do you feel about these words?
- How might you better express your faith with others?

*Christ, the Morning Star, came back from the dead and shed his peaceful light on all the earth. (Exultet)*
- How do you experience Christ's peaceful light?
- What areas of your life most need this light?

*Stay with us, Lord, for it is almost evening and the day is nearly over. (Luke 24)*
- Spend time now reflecting on this plea of the disciples on the road to Emmaus.
- What do you want to say to Jesus as he blesses you?

Chapter 8

# Running beside the Cross

> Let us run with perseverance
> the race that is set before us.
>
> —*Hebrews 12:1*

The cross is always part of our journey to the Father. Pain, suffering, and death are a natural part of our existence. But understanding of the purpose of the cross in our lives is another matter altogether. We struggle to make sense of the mystery of suffering.

How can we incorporate the mystery of the cross into our daily lives? Let me share an example based on one of my "ordinary" days on the golf course. Those who know me well might think that golf is my best game. But is it? On this particular day I had to think seriously about whether golf was indeed my best game. I was enjoying my best score on the course this year, but on the second hole I sprained my ankle going through the trees to look for my ball on another fairway. After that I hobbled a bit but kept gamely tried to "work it out" by walking and running a couple of miles on my ankle.

The pain was making me philosophic. Earlier that morning I had been visiting a ninety-one-year-old recently-widowed friend. The time to sit and sip and visit had been very precious. This was surely one of God's finest people! At the time I had been balancing this visit against the time for writing and my exercise. The more I think about it now, the more I realize that golf was not my best game, was not the most important game of the day!

The pain continued to eat away at my consciousness, even though I made some great chip shots and barely missed a couple of birdies. So what was my best game today? I realized that I had to endure the pain of the ankle and offer it as a prayer for the sick and lonely members of my community. As the afternoon progressed, so did my discomfort. I was using ice packs by suppertime. Had I miscalculated on the degree of injury in trying to work it out? It didn't really matter. I had been pondering the meaning of pain earlier in the morning as my friend told me about her husband's last days with her. He was in such pain that she couldn't touch him as he lay on his bed. The Lord had finally taken him to the place where there is no more pain and no more tears. Now she feels some relief on his behalf, though she misses him dearly and needs her friends to support her.

Golf was certainly not my most important game that day, nor was it my best. I had led a communion service with our parish prayer team at 9:00 that morning, and later I was part of the "visiting team" that took me to my friend. For a short time and in a very limited way, I had then shared in "the suffering of the saints." I count myself blessed that the Lord asked me to sit on the bench with an ice pack later in the day and to cast (I use this word with caution) a reflective eye on my present and future career as a player.

## Signs of Aging

There is a less than flippant side to aging, and that is the aches and pains in the joints, failing health, and sometimes disappointments in our expectations for our lives. It is often difficult to appreciate the beauty that surrounds us as we struggle on life's journey. Recently I was reflecting on aging, and I realized that as we get older, our birthday suits get heavier. Eventually they will need ironing.

Red Skelton said there were three ages: youth, middle age, and "you look good." In the movie *Revenge of a Middle-Aged Woman*, a character says, "I'm shrinking a half inch a year. If I live to be eighty, I'll be as high as a coffee table."

I recently wrote an article on aging. In it I referred to the T-shirt slogan celebrating age: "The older I get the better I was."

The article included these "signs of aging":

Your knees buckle, but your belt won't.

Your back goes out more than you do.

You sink your teeth into a steak and they stay there.

Your children are beginning to look middle-aged.

And the clincher was: "It's scary when you start making the same noise as your coffee maker."

Remember, "You don't stop laughing because you grow old; you grow old because you stop laughing."

At the personal level, I believe there is much in the aging process to give us hope and not despair, laughter as well as tears. One sad fact as we get older is that we can sometimes lose sight of what we have done well. It would be sad if the saying "The older I get the better I was" were true. The truth should be: the older I get, the better I am.

Just last week I visited an elderly man, now in a wheel chair, who is very frustrated with his state in life. He is in effect saying, "Why bother to eat? There is nothing to do. You have to wait and wait. What's the point?" The point is that he has perhaps lost sight of all the good works of his earlier life. Often parents who have sacrificed heroically for their children may feel useless after their children leave home. Fruitful careers are sometimes forgotten in the idleness and unimportance of non-work. Yet, "God is not unjust and will not overlook your work and the love you have shown in serving the saints as you still do" (Hebrews 6:10). My point is that

**We are more creatures of light than of darkness.**

we are more creatures of light than of darkness. "I live by faith in the Son of God, who loved me and sacrificed himself for me" (Galatians 2:20). "Your light is a lamp for my feet and a light on my path" (Psalm 119:105).

As I was preparing this chapter I did a quick check in my home. I could readily count at least fifty functional bulbs to light my days and nights. There is a certain security in having light. But I had to wonder: how many spiritual "lights" do I have? How many times a day do I tap into God's spiritual light? Scripture tells us that the Word is the true light that enlightens us all (John 1:9). All the lamps in our homes pale when placed beside the light of Christ that guides us through the dark night of death and the shadow of our fallen nature. Christ is light. "I am the light of the world; anyone who follows me will not be walking in the dark; but will have the light of life" (John 8:12). Divine light fills our lives with grace. It enables us to truly realize the significance of our lives as we live them.

### Filled with Light

I remember one June morning in high school. Before I entered the building to take an exam, a classmate came up to me and said, "You look like you know everything." That is a description of our lives when we are filled with God's light. Rejoice and believe the good news!

During a difficult week recently, when stresses and struggles were no longer a memory of more youthful days, I did realize the joy of God's handiwork. Walking home at night after a meeting, I noticed how the trees created an arch in the light of the street lamps, and how the moon cast a brightness beyond. During the day, the same scene was as enthralling with the golden September leaves. We please God when we are fully alive to all that is beautiful around us. Love of creation is the highest thanks we can give to the creator.

*Talk about Troubles!*

One of my favorite Bible passages, which illustrates vision beyond the suffering and trials of this life, is from Job 19. Talk about troubles! In one day the Sabeans killed Job's servants and stole his donkeys; the sheep and more servants were burned in a fire that fell from heaven; the Chaldeans carried off the camels and killed more servants; and even Job's sons and daughters, who were feasting at the eldest brother's house, were killed when the house fell on them. Job still worshiped the Lord saying, "Naked I came from my mother's womb, and naked shall I return there; the Lord gave and the Lord has taken away; blessed be the name of the Lord." Job was a man of great faith. He was so convinced of the eternal realities and our life in heaven that even after all his trials he said: "O that my words were written down! And that they were inscribed in a book! O that with an iron pen and with lead they were engraved on a rock forever! For I know that my Redeemer lives, and that at the last…in my flesh I shall see God" (Job 19:23–26).

We are much more fortunate than Job. Jesus came among us and experienced our world and our suffering. He is sympathetic with our plight. He lived, prayed, suffered, and died as a vulnerable human being. Through his cross he made it possible to laugh in the face of the gloom, despair, and agony in our lives. German scholar Jurgen Moltmann writes about the image of God on the cross: "God is not greater than he is in this humiliation. God is not more glorious than he is in this self-surrender. God is not more powerful than he is in this helplessness. God is not more divine than he is in this humanity." And later he says, "The proof of God's love is in the cross—contemplate it. This is not a God of indifference, as the agnostics/atheist would state."

Many today find it easy to turn their beliefs away from a God who has created a world in which suffering occurs. Many see God as indifferent to pain and injustice. "Sometimes we picture him lounging, perhaps dozing, in some celestial deck-chair. We think of him as an armchair spectator, almost gloating over the world's suffering, and enjoying his own isolation from it" (John Stott, *The Cross of Christ*, pp. 330-336). Nothing could be further from the truth! I repeat, nothing could be further from the truth. Stott continues: "He [God] entered our world of flesh and blood, tears and death. He suffered for us. Our sufferings become more manageable in the light of his. There is still a question mark about human suffering, but over it we boldly stamp another mark, the cross which symbolizes divine suffering."

## A Tangible Sign

The cross of Christ is a tangible sign of God's vested interest in our suffering. Contemplating the cross, we at once see its eternal significance and its power to transform us. Just as the Hebrews (Numbers 21:9) looked on the serpent on the pole and were physically healed, we can look on the cross of Christ and be moved by the power of Christ's love.

Contemplating the cross brings us closer to the love that is still pouring out for us from a God who has given himself to us. As the psalmist puts it, "I keep Yahweh before me always, for with him at my right hand, nothing can shake me" (Psalm 16:8). We need to seek the love poured out for us on the cross. It is powerful enough to help us withstand the pain, suffering, and even death that we face in this world.

In our limited vision we do often blame God for our problems. We wonder: what sense does it make that often sinners prosper and saints suffer? Suffering and death often beset us when we are least able to endure them. We may be close to a spiritual balance that makes sense of it all when age or infirmity deals us a staggering blow. We are like boxers who have learned to face our opponent, but then suddenly are overwhelmed by a superior force. When we are not strong any more, the blows come.

Because we are only human, we tend to focus on pain and suffering, often one short step from melancholy and despair. Our greatest mystics have struggled with what John of the Cross calls the "dark night of the soul." Even Mother Teresa struggled with feelings of abandonment; at times feeling rejected by God, helpless, and tempted to abandon her work.

> We can look on the cross of Christ and be moved by the power of Christ's love.

We have well-known names for the places of agony and crucifixion: Gethsemani and Calvary. Most people know of them. But ask the next ten people you meet if they can name the place of the resurrection.

To many it is a stranger's tomb, a borrowed and forgotten place, unless they have toured the Holy Land and visited the Church of the Holy Sepulchre.

We have to remind ourselves that pain is a spiritual process. It can be a spiritual experience. Even if we lack the passion of the martyrs who sang as they suffered, we can accept that Christ's sacrifice has something to do with this spiritual process. Our suffering and the sickness and pain we endure in this world can sanctify us and, united to the suffering of Christ, add to the eventual and total victory of good over evil.

Our God is a God of hope. Jesus came to point us to that future where evil will be defeated. Satan will never overcome God. It may not seem so to the person facing death or pain, but we have Jesus' promise that the gates of hell will never prevail. And Jesus has gone before us, in our shoes, to open the hates of heaven.

Jesus came to bring forgiveness for our failings as we struggle toward greatness. We need to forgive ourselves even as we pray: "forgive us our trespasses as we forgive those who trespass against us." Forgive me Lord when I don't understand your plan. Forgive me when I hide from you and your cross.

## Hiding His Faith

*A friend was in front of me coming out of church one day, and the preacher was standing at the door as he always does to shake hands.*

*He grabbed my friend by the hand and pulled him aside. The Pastor said, "You need to join the army of the Lord!"*

*My friend said, "I'm already in the army of the Lord, Pastor."*

*But the Pastor questioned, "How come I don't see you except at Christmas and Easter?"*

*My friend whispered back, "I'm in the Secret Service."*

—Internet, Source Unknown

## A Graced Experience

I had a grace experience this year on the feast of Christ the King. In our liturgy we celebrate this feast on the last Sunday before Advent. With our pastor away, I was asked to do a reflection for a lay service. I was somewhat taken aback by the readings for the day. The gospel was from Luke 23:35–43 and dealt with Christ on the cross being ridiculed by the thief. Golgotha! Calvary! The execution of Jesus. This was a strange kingship. To the thief on his right Christ says: "Today you will be with me in Paradise." Now that struck me as a proclamation a king might make. Certainly we all need the mercy of this king as much as the thief on the cross did.

I struggled on with the preparation and researched how the site of the crucifixion has been claimed by different groups over the centuries. Ironically, it has had pagan temples built on it as well as Christian basilicas. Persians, Moslems, and Christians have disputed over the territory. Today many believe the Church of the Holy Sepulcher is on or as near as possible to the actual place of crucifixion. But then I found a story that I decided to use instead. It says so much about the kingship of Christ that no other words were necessary.

## You Have Done It to Me

There was a young lady named Sally who relates an experience she had in a college theology class with a teacher called Brother Smith. Brother Smith was known for his elaborate object lessons. One day when Sally entered the class, there was a big target on the wall, and on a nearby table there were darts. Brother Smith told the students to draw a picture of someone they disliked or someone who had made them angry, and he would allow them to throw darts at that person's picture.

Sally drew a picture of Brother Smith himself, putting a great deal of detail into her drawing, even drawing pimples on his face. Sally was pleased at the overall effect she had achieved. The class lined up and began throwing darts with much laughter and hilarity. Some of the students threw their darts with such force that their targets were ripping apart. Sally looked forward to her turn, and was disappointed when Brother Smith asked the students to return to their seats early. As Sally sat thinking about how angry she was because she didn't have a chance to throw any darts at her target, Brother Smith began removing the target from the wall.

Underneath the target was a picture of Jesus. A complete hush fell over the room as each student viewed the mangled picture of Jesus; holes and jagged marks covered his face, and his eyes were pierced out. Brother Smith said only these words, "In as much as you have done it to the least of these, you have done it to me." No other words were necessary; the tear-filled eyes of each student focused only on the picture of Christ. The students remained in their seats even after the bell rang. Finally they left the classroom, tears streaming down their faces.

Yet, the thought of eternal reward and punishment still makes us uneasy. What's it all about? A homilist recently described his idea of heaven as a place where you serve and are served. It is not a place where you have everything that you could want or wish for. As children, we imagined this to mean all the ice cream or candy we could eat and still want more. If heaven is ice cream and candy, it is an empty heaven!

## A Place of Service

A visionary once described hell as a place where everyone was seated at a great banquet table laden with "gorgeous" food. The problem was that everyone had a spoon that was two feet long. Try as they might, they could not get a mouthful for themselves. Right next door was heaven—same scene, same food, same spoons. Only here everyone was busy feeding one another. This was a full and active heaven! Love does not stop in heaven!

I had a dream recently that left me with the inspiration that everyone can be Christ to someone else. The dream started in a rather odd way: I was lending my cross-country skis to my oldest brother. I tried to advise him to be careful so he wouldn't twist a knee or ankle. I woke up shortly after with a head cold and some congestion, and on inspiration, offered up the discomfort for him. Perhaps he had come to mind for a reason. Then, in the twilight of sleep, I imagined a Thursday morning liturgy at the Lodge, the local seniors care center. The challenge to the homilist was to show how everyone there could be Christ to others. The staff certainly can be Christ as they minister to the patients and assist each other. The doctors and nurses can be in the front line administering aid and often spending extra time and effort far beyond the call of duty. Then there are the family members and other visitors who administer loving time and attention: "I was sick and in prison, and you visited me."

The biggest challenge, if you haven't noticed it yet, still remained to be met. How can the sick and the suffering be Jesus Christ to everyone else? In a profound way the sick, the dying, the suffering are the body of the suffering Christ. Tending them is touching the body of Christ. Suffering is something of a mystery, but we know that it can be a chance to really share in the cross of Christ and to offer that up for others. There is no long line forming at the cross. Even Christ, the night before his death, asked the Father if this cup could pass away without his drinking it. Ultimately, we need to also say, "Your will be done," as we accept suffering and death in our lives.

Suffering is part of the human condition. Sometimes when it gets to be too much, we can cry out to Jesus for help and he comes to our assistance. Suffering can make us the most like Jesus; it is being on the cross with him. Offering our suffering as prayer is truly partaking in the cross and its redemptive power for others and us.

Suffering can be a chance to really share in the cross of Christ.

Jesus' own final suffering took place in Jerusalem. The very word conjures up images and emotions that affect us deeply. To some the word "Jerusalem" brings to mind a Swedish rock band, or a foreign-language film, a Yom Kippur celebration: "next year in Jerusalem," a divided city with Palestinian and Jewish residents, a holy city where Jews, Muslims, and Christians co-exist. When you look at a timeline of political occupation of Jerusalem, the mere history of it is numbing. Starting in 1,000 B.C. with King David, we move through some familiar names: Solomon, Pompey, Pilate, and Constantine; the Persian, Greek, and Roman (birth of Christ) occupations; the Byzantine, Muslim, and Ottoman Empires; even Napoleon (invaded Palestine); and to the British mandate 1917–1948. Since then we have seen Israeli rulers: Ben Gurian, Golda Meir, Moshe Dayon, Begin, Rabin, Netanyahu, Baruk, and Ariel Sharon.

Jerusalem has been called the place where heaven meets earth. Holy to Jews, Christians, and Muslims alike, the alluring city of Jerusalem has withstood the adversities of myriad wars and conflicts only to emerge today as a thriving center rich in history, religion, and culture. Believed to be the link between the physical world and that of faith and ideas, this Holy City has been both celebrated and desecrated many times over. Its ancient name, Salem (after the pagan deity of the city), is connected with the words *Shalom* in Hebrew and *Salaam* in Arabic.

## The New Jerusalem

Lately I have been thinking of the New Jerusalem, a symbolic description of the place where God's love dwells in fullness; where there is peace on Jerusalem's borders, and where the Lord feeds her inhabitants with finest wheat (Psalm 147:12–14). In Hebrews 12:21–24 we read of "Mount Zion and the city of the living God, the heavenly Jerusalem where the millions of angels have gathered for the festival, with the whole Church in which everyone is a 'first-born son' and a citizen of heaven." This mystical place is our future as God's kingdom is established. And this is our job, our challenge: How do we bring about the "New Jerusalem"?

Jesus proclaimed, "This is my commandment: love one another." God is Love. We become like God as we become love. "Whoever sees me sees the one who sent me…for I have come not to judge the world, but to save the world" (John 12:45–48). In 1 John 4:16–17, we hear that "God is love and all who live in love live in God, and God lives in them. Love will come to its perfection in us when we can face the day of judgment without fear; because even in this world we have become as he is."

Near the end of 1 John we read: "I have written all this to you so that you who believe in the name of the Son of God may be sure that you have eternal life." Let us continue to develop our relationship with God by serving him with sincere hearts. By getting to know him we assure ourselves of his promise: "…for they shall all know me, from the least of them to the greatest. For I will be merciful towards their iniquities, and I will remember their sins no more" (Hebrews 8:11–12). Just after Jesus dies on the cross in Mel Gibson's *The Passion of the Christ*, what appears to be a giant teardrop falls from heaven and strikes the earth. In the filming of this story, the camera has several times viewed the scene from above, from the vantage point of God. It is also a unique experience to view the events of the crucifixion from the point of view of the cross. I had that experience recently again in rehearsing *The*

*Mystery of the Passion of Christ* and was asked to fill in for Jesus. I was struck by some of the thoughts Jesus might have had from this unusual vantage point. I share these with you here.

Here is my Mother Mary looking up at me. "See, Mother, I make all things new." What I notice most is her open eyes, pools of her soul. Her look is asking, but she is trusting. Beside her is John, who is an open book. He has much to say about love. "Mother, behold, he is your son. Son, she is your mother." It's hard to focus through this wall of pain. My shoulder is in flames. Why is it not numb like my back? "My God, my God, why have you forsaken me?" It's thick and black, this wall of pain. The eyes of the flesh are swollen and blind; the eyes of faith are clear.

There is Simon, who was compelled to help me carry the cross or I would have expired on the way. His first reaction was, "All right, but I'm an innocent man, forced to carry the cross of a condemned man" (from *The Passion of the Christ*). Now he is changed forever.

The soldiers, they mock me. They are like children with their self-centered taunts. "Father forgive them; they do not know what they are doing." They deride me: "Save yourself!" "If you come down now, I will believe you!" "Hail, King of the Jews!" If they only knew how much I love them. I really want to save them but they are shutting me out. I forgive them. I am dying for them. I really want to love them, to open their hearts.

"I am thirsty." Through the darkening fog the soldier gives me a sponge soaked in wine. I refuse to drink. I do not want to be drugged. Someone is calling me. "Jesus, remember me when you come into your kingdom." I try to turn to the right, but it is a blur of pain. I can see his faith. "I tell you, Dismas, today you will be with me in Paradise." There is also someone on the cross to my left. He needs the salvation of my blood to free him. I really want to love him, to forgive him. I hear the cry of his heart.

The darkness is closing in. "Father, into your hands I commend my spirit."

 For Your Reflection

*Your word is a lamp to my feet and a light to my path. (Psalm 119:105)*
- Is God's word a companion on your journey?
- How might it become even more so?

*The Lord gave and the Lord has taken away. Blessed be the name of the Lord. (Job 1:20)*
- What in your life have you considered a blessing from God?
- What has been taken away? Are you still able to give praise?

*I will be merciful through their iniquities, and I will remember their sins no more. (Hebrews 8:11–12)*
- Ponder these words today and take them to heart.

# Chapter 9

# Running into God's Arms

*God loves us. In our darkest moments,
God is there for us, waiting with open arms,
inviting us to run into them.*

A very dear friend of mine is dying of cancer. I took Communion to him this afternoon. Several times today I have been struck by the thought that he is lying on his hospital bed about the business of dying, while I am in my house about the business of living, in the flesh, with its appetites and hungers and its aversion to things of death.

This friend has been an inspiration to me with his energy to serve. Even cancer couldn't stop him from being at services every morning until last week, ready to do the readings of the day, lead the rosary, or lead a lay service if required. He always said, "I'll do it, Ken, while I can. When I'm gone you'll have to do it." I am sure the Lord is waiting for him with open arms. In John's vision in

Revelation, he sees a door open in heaven and hears a voice speaking to him like a trumpet saying, "Come up here: I will show you what is to come in the future" (Revelation 4:1). He could be speaking to my friend.

God loves us and in our darkest moments is there for us, his angels at our sides. Knowing God's love for us transforms us. We join the heavenly chorus and cry out, "Holy, Holy, Holy is the Lord God, the almighty; he was, he is, he is to come" (Revelations 4:8). I have a clear vision of my friend at heaven's gate, and the Lord is calling him. His frail and wasted body will be restored and sadness will flee away. Sweet Savior, haste!

## We Still Fear

Yet, our human nature fears this moment. Fear is something we have all experienced in our lives starting with first memories. As a child I remember being afraid of the dark. There were monsters under the bed and in the closet. I remember crossing the farm yard one winter night and looking over my shoulder to see a shadowy figure, the family dog, bounding over a snow bank. I imagine it was as scary as the experience of my older brother jogging at night on a country road when a horse snorted in the ditch behind him. As a college student, I was still looking over my shoulder as I walked on city streets at night.

The good news is that we do not need to fear because we have a sure hope that Jesus, "a forerunner on our behalf," has entered death before us (Hebrews 6:20). It is a matter of faith. If we have just a little mustard seed of faith we could move mountains (Matthew 13:31). With faith, we believe that God nourishes us spiritually and transforms our fears.

Through faith, our human condition with all its weaknesses and flaws, its imperfections, is elevated to become Christ. We become children of God. It is possible for us to be Christ to our neighbor, to herald the good news, to celebrate with our brothers and sisters in what is a foretaste of the heavenly banquet. We would be foolish to struggle along life's challenging journey without proper nourishment. There is nothing preventing us from living our lives in confidence and joy, dining on rich spiritual food from wellsprings of grace provided by Christ in his church. It has all been "paid for" already at a tremendous price. How our lives will change when we accept God's abundant grace. We will have no fear of the dark night of death. Evil will frighten us no longer. Life's challenges will be viewed against an infinite horizon.

Ask the Lord for the help that is assured.

Isaiah (8:22–23) describes the wanderer in darkness: "distressed…he will wander through the country starving, he will become frenzied [the pleasure-seeking frenzied world that never satisfies]…and will see nothing at night. Is not all blackness where anguish is?" Contrast this with the hope of Christ, "I, the light, have come into the world, so whoever believes in me need not stay in the dark anymore" (John 12:46). "Walk while you have light, or dark will overtake you; those who walk in the dark do not know where they are going. While you have the light, believe in the light and you will become children of light" (John 12:35–36). Come back to the Father while you have a grain of faith. Do not wait for the darkness to close in. Ask the Lord for the help that is assured. Burdens become light with faith. Fear not. God's light is breaking through the darkness of sin and division. "The people that walked in darkness has seen a great light; on those who live in a land of deep shadows, a light has shone" (Isaiah 9:3).

### The Gift of Sight

Our appreciation of sight is something we take for granted. Imagine the shadows of blindness! At nineteen months of age, Helen Keller was stricken with an illness that left her deaf and blind. Eventually she learned to read by Braille, went to college, became a famous author, and lectured internationally. I wonder what she could have accomplished had she been able to see and hear like you and me.

In Mark 10, we read the story of Bartimaeus, a blind beggar sitting by the roadside listening until he hears the sound he has been waiting for, the sound of a passing rabbi named Jesus. Bartimaeus throws off his cloak and springs up to meet Jesus. Bartimaeus' story has several levels of meaning. At the simple, literal level we see a man who has heard about Jesus, has believed what he heard, and has waited a long time for the "chance of a lifetime," that Jesus would be passing by in his world of darkness.

Imagine what joy dawned in his heart as he heard the voices, the footfalls coming nearer. Bartimaeus was so sure in his faith that he threw off his cloak and sprang toward Jesus. Imagine how many nights he must have clutched that coat to himself for security and warmth. Imagine that leap of faith! Imagine the long-awaited light filling his eyes in a miraculous flash! What followed leads us to deeper reflection. Bartimaeus left everything else and followed Jesus.

When you and I receive our spiritual eyesight we are ready to follow Jesus, rejoicing. But, like Bartimaeus, we first need to call out, "Jesus, Son of David, have mercy on me!" This simple prayer is echoed when the lepers cry out, "Jesus, Master, have mercy on us!" (Luke 17:13), and when the tax collector pleads, "God, be merciful to me, a sinner" (18:13). This is the core of an ancient prayer called the Jesus Prayer. It originated in Eastern Christianity and is described in *The Way of the Pilgrim*.

The Jesus Prayer came about because a man wanted to learn a simple prayer he could repeat over and over, even as he went about his daily work. "Lord Jesus Christ, Son of God, have mercy on me, a sinner."

## On the Lighter Side

I remember a neighbor on our farm describing a Russian-German friend of his who could roll a cigarette with one hand. He did this once while seated on a horse. He forgot one thing, however; as he rolled the paper, the crisp crackling (*rascheln*) sound sent the horse into a furious buck. "*Got sei mir sinder gneddig hot der gawl gebocked!*" ("God be merciful to me, a sinner! Did that horse buck!"), the neighbor exclaimed, an indication of how deeply ingrained the Jesus Prayer is in the folk culture of the Russian people.

The Jesus Prayer is a perfect profession of faith. By saying it, we are confessing our sinfulness, crying out for God's mercy, and asking for God's direct intervention in our lives.

In our world today there are many, many people sitting by the roadside listening, waiting, praying for the footsteps of Jesus to come along. Some have waited a long, long time in the dark. That's where you and I come in. We are the hands and feet of Jesus. We are his voice and even his presence. We walk with the eyes of faith in the light, in his light!

## Close To God

We are closer to God than we think. Sometimes the thin veil separating us from the eternal, from God, is transparent or even removed. We know from scripture that at the death of Jesus, "the veil of the temple was torn in two from top to bottom" (Matthew 27:51). The veil that separated the high priests and prophets from their Lord was removed in a real sense, though it is easier for us to see only its symbolism. Jesus reached through the veil that separates us in this world from the eternal. In him we can trust. "Here we have an anchor for our soul, as sure as it is firm, and reaching right through beyond the veil where Jesus has entered before us and on our behalf" (Hebrews 6:19).

This past week I was approached in the store by a lady who asked me, "Are you the one who writes the articles in the paper?"

"Yes," I said. Then she related this story to me. She went to visit her friend who was dying of lung cancer. As she entered the hospital room she thought, "Oh, is she suffering." Just then, in a split second, she could no longer see her friend. She saw the face of Jesus. He was looking down and smiling. She felt a great calm and peace.

As noted earlier, I have been present at the death of one of God's loved ones, and I have witnessed what can only have been a vision of what lies beyond this veil separating our world from the eternal. As my mother lay dying, a smile replaced the pain in her face, and she was suddenly and completely at peace. And as he lay dying, my Father-in-law lifted his head and fixed his gaze on a vision that he saw beyond the presence of family members in the room.

We can travel in faith with our Lord Jesus who set his face like flint as he traveled to Jerusalem. Let us be sure of our purpose and direction as we renew our spiritual roots. Now is a time of conversion, as we take a few scriptural steps toward our final goal. Jesus came, "To bring the good news to the poor…set the downtrodden free" (Luke 4:18–19). Are we listening? Are we open to his call? His truth will set us free.

Jesus said, "I am the gate of the sheepfold. Anyone who enters through me will be safe. I have come so that you may have life and have it to the full. I am the good shepherd who lays down his life for his sheep" (John 14:2–3). And later to show us his love, "I am going to prepare a place for you; I shall return to take you with me" (John 11:2–3). Let us be ready to accept Christ's promise: "I am the resurrection. Those who believe in me, even though they die will live. And whoever believes in me will never die" (John 11:25–26).

## Not in Silence

I have often had this daydream. Suppose I were about to die and had a chance to write a brief message on a slip of paper or in the dust, what would it be? One that has come to mind is, "Come in peace." Today I might amend that and add, "but not in silence." As

Jesus was entering Jerusalem, the whole group of disciples was praising him at the tops of their voices. When the Pharisees asked Jesus to check his disciples, Jesus said, "I tell you, if these keep silence the stones will cry out" (Luke 19:40). We must not be silent!

## Speak Up

*A man traveled all around the world, often stopping to buy something for his mother. Once he bought her a parrot that spoke thirty different languages. He called his mother, "Did you like the parrot?" he asked her.*

*"Oh yes," she replied. "It was delicious."*

*"What?!" the man cried. "You ate it! That parrot wasn't for you to eat! It spoke thirty languages!"*

*The mother paused and then said, "So why didn't he say something?"*

The purpose of this joke is to focus our attention on silence. Silence can be a good thing (though not for the parrot). When Elijah was looking for the Lord, he found him in the sound of a gentle breeze (1 Kings 19:12–13). As baptized Christians infused with the Holy Spirit, we definitely have something to shout about! And we have many models who show us how to do the shouting. Let me share three examples.

1. Mother Teresa was once asked about the simplest way ordinary people can help others. "By smiling at one another," she said. Small acts of kindness and love, our smiles and goodwill, are what transform the world.

2. As a child I remember driving to school by closed cutter (sleigh) in winter. Those January mornings were cold and gloomy. I remember that my sister Helen was always cheerful and joking. Her attitude positively affected the rest of us. Later God called her to religious life and has since called her to her eternal reward. Her cheerful smile left an impression on her community, on the youth she worked with, and on her family members.

*Thanks to the presence of the Holy Spirit, we can carry on a loving relationship with God.*

3. St. Seraphim of Sarov was one of the three saints described in *Crossing the Threshold* by John Paul II. Even after the death of St. Seraphim in 1833, stories of his miracles continued. "Soldiers were greeted by a smiling little man in a white smock, lost travelers guided in howling blizzards by a little man in white." "He is one of ours," Mary said to Saints Peter and Paul who accompanied her in an apparition to Seraphim, who once spent a thousand continuous days and nights in prayer in his monastery.

He was close to forest animals. One visitor watched as a big black bear ate from the monk's hand, while his face was described as "joyous and bright, as that of an angel." Thousands came from all over Russia to visit Seraphim the monk. He called each one "my joy" and hailed them with the Easter greeting "Christ is Risen!" He was a spiritual counselor with the gift to read hearts. In one carefully recorded passage the monk addressed the unspoken question of a friend who wanted to know the true aim of Christian life. Seraphim explained that it consists of "acquiring the Holy Spirit." As these words were spoken, the friend recalls that a blinding light spread around for several yards. "See, my son, what unspeakable joy the Lord has now granted us!" Seraphim exclaimed as waves and waves of light, warmth, heavenly fragrance, joy, and peace surrounded them.

Recently I listened to a motivational speaker who challenged a group of retired teachers with a formula for living that is worth considering at any age. "Set long-term goals," he said. Look at what you want to be in ten years; look at what you want to accomplish in the next two years, and look at your immediate plans and how they will start you on that journey to success. That sounds simple enough: decide what you want, what needs to be done, prioritize and start. "It's okay to say it's too hard," he said, "but so many people quit just before success comes. There is no such thing as failure; learn to 'fail forward,'" he advised. One of his challenges is to invite people to write an obituary that, at the time of death, will describe the successes in their lives. Then, when they know what they want to become, they can begin the course that will take them there.

I mused on this sage advice and realized that there is an application to our spiritual lives. We know where we want to be when our lives end, and now we need to begin the process that will get us there. My advice is to go with passion. Whatever lesser desires may seem to drive us, we have higher passions that will override them. God is more important than our weaknesses. Love of God has to be our overwhelming passion. When we have this worthwhile goal, we will be ready to sacrifice and work toward it. We can do hard things. Today's failure may be tomorrow's opportunity. Go with passion! Enjoy the "gifts" of the Creator.

St. Francis of Assisi lived his life with passion. He once said, "Preach the gospel at all times. Use words if necessary." God our Father loves us so much that he sent his son to give us a God who understands our nature, a God we can touch physically. But since Jesus rose from the dead and ascended into heaven, we need some other real presence of God's love in our world, and so God sent the Spirit to be in touch with our daily situation.

Thanks to the presence of the Holy Spirit, we can carry on a loving relationship with God. When we lift our hearts to God in the affairs of everyday life, we know the loving comfort such a relationship can bring. It is like a son or daughter leaving home and being in touch with the parent by telephone or computer. It takes a mere fraction of a second to be there, to see and hear. Today, for example, using a web cam I was able to communicate by audio and video with my daughter and son-in-law in Thunder Bay. My daughter pointed the camera out the window and showed me Lake Head Campus and areas of the city. Communication with God is even simpler than this.

## The Burden Is Lifted

What we look forward to after our Gethsemane and Calvary experiences is a joyous union with the resurrected Christ, a laughing Christ at the banquet table of the heavenly feast. The heavy burden of sin has been lifted by his death, and all we have to do is believe and turn to him. What is the reward for "turning to the Lord"? Dismas, a thief on the cross beside Christ, received what no other on earth has ever received—the promise that "…today you will be with me in Paradise" (Luke 23:43). That promise is meant for all of us. "God loved the world so much that he gave his only Son, so that everyone who believes in him may not be lost but may have eternal life"(John 3:16). No one who believes in him will be condemned.

Lift up your hearts! I say again, rejoice. As Judas in the Passion play, I have the role of attempting repentance for my betrayal of Christ. The role is a challenge. How do you portray a guilt-ridden mad man, moments before he hangs himself? With much anguish and gnashing of teeth. After the play, I truly need to contemplate the resurrection. The miracle of the resurrection changed everything: in the fraction of a second, in that millisecond, human history and creation changed forever! As the Exultet proclaims: "Rejoice, heavenly power! Sing choirs of angels! Rejoice, O earth, in shining splendor…; Darkness vanishes forever!"

We are not left alone on our spiritual journey. Just as the risen Jesus met many times with his disciples before his Ascension, to instruct and lead them, in the same way his Holy Spirit works in us, his church, to inspire and instruct. The Spirit has not left us orphaned. What a rich spiritual treasure we have!

## Spiritual Gold

Imagine being caught up in the fever of the California Gold Rush. You could be swept along to the place where you could find millions in gold (this appeals to the Judas in me). Digging deeper would reveal more gold. What a time to celebrate! St. John of the

Cross in *Spiritual Canticle* tells us that for the rest of our lives we can dig ever more deeply into the treasure that is Christ revealed to us: "He is like a rich mine with many pockets containing treasure; however deep we dig we will never find their end or their limit."

Heaven starts in the heart.

Recently my wife and I had the privilege of flying to Thunder Bay to visit our daughter. As we flew above the Canadian landscape at 37,000 feet and later, because of thunderclouds below us, at 47,000 feet, I felt very close to God. It seemed a privilege to be in a position of looking down at the earth and seeing it as perhaps God might. It was like a retreat. I knew I'd be coming back down to earth, literally and figuratively, but I really felt close to God. I thought of the afterlife and what joy there will be. It was almost like a transfiguration. I could practically see angels on the wings of the jet. I certainly sensed the love of Jesus and the joy we anticipate at that final banquet of love when the servant of all will be attending us.

I was reading a great book at the time, *The Jesus I Never Knew* by Philip Yancey, and he was talking about this very experience of the happy afterlife Jesus promised his followers. When you are above the clouds, eight miles high, some thoughts become crystal clear, some abstractions easier. Maybe it is because of the nearness of where we assume heaven to be. But heaven starts in the heart. It grows in the joy of loving service to others and in accepting their love in return. That part of heaven starts on earth as we continue our lives of prayer and service.

My wish for you is that you will have many of your own close-to-God experiences on your life journey. May you continue running the good race until that day when you run into the welcoming arms of our loving God. May you leap with the joy of resurrection and never look back.

 For Your Reflection

*Jesus, a "forerunner on our behalf" has entered death before us. (Hebrew 6:20)*
- Have you thought of Jesus as one who runs before you?
- How does it feel to know he is beside you?

*While you have the light, believe in the light, and you will become children of light. (John 12:35–36)*
- Do you experience God's presence as light in your life?
- In what ways are you a child of the light?

*Lord Jesus Christ, Son of the Living God, have mercy on me. (Jesus Prayer)*
- Have you ever prayed this or a similar prayer?
- What do the words say to you?

*I have come so that you may have life and have it to the full. (John 14:2–3)*
- Are you preparing for the fullness of life?
- What does this mean in your life right now?